MUSICIANS INSTITUTE

ESSENTIAL CONCEPTS

HARMONY
& THEORY

by Keith Wyatt & Carl Schroeder

ISBN 0-7935-7991-0

HAL•LEONARD®
CORPORATION

7777 W. BLUEMOUND RD. P.O. BOX 13819 MILWAUKEE, WI 53213

Visit Hal Leonard Online at
www.halleonard.com

ESSENTIAL CONCEPTS

HARMONY & THEORY

Contents

The Theory
of
Love

Wendell Novotny

Introduction

The chart on the facing page tells a complete story, but it's a story written in a special language: the language of music. It contains information that allows any two musicians anywhere on this planet, speaking entirely different languages with their tongues, to play the same piece of music on their instruments. To musicians who know the language, charts like this are the beginning point of musical conversation; to those who don't, they are just a lot of meaningless numbers and symbols. If this chart looks more confusing than enlightening, this book is for you.

Harmony and Theory evolved through years of writing, teaching, and revising the course of the same name at Musicians Institute. MI is a hands-on musical performance school that emphasizes the stage, not the classroom, so in this context the reason for studying harmony and theory is practical, not intellectual. The goal of the course is simply to enable anyone playing any instrument in any popular style to pick up a book of sheet music and understand what they see. The point is to know the language well enough that you don't have to stop playing while you think about it—to be able to use it as a tool to help you think more musically and thereby play better, quicker. As such, the knowledge contained in this book doesn't replace good instrumental technique, playing experience, an accurate ear, or a sense of style, but it does provide a structure to tie all of those essentials together, making you a complete musician.

Most harmony and theory books approach the subject from a classical or composition-oriented perspective, but this one is for those whose first love is playing popular music in all its variations—rock, funk, blues, pop, country, jazz, etc. Many, if not most, popular musicians first learn to play by ear and by feel, copying what others have done without necessarily knowing why it works. "Ear" and "feel" players also tend to be very unsure about the virtue of studying theory, caught between a sense of frustration at being musically illiterate and a fear that too much knowledge will get in the way of natural inspiration. Well-rounded musicians, however, learn to use their intellect to focus and enhance their creativity, much as an artist studies the inside of the human body in order to be better able to paint the outside. This book is intended to give you an understanding of the internal structure of everyday music so that instead of shying away from the printed page you can read it and get past it, back to the music itself.

As teachers and authors, we have made a great many choices regarding what to put into this book and what to leave out. New concepts are introduced by showing how and why they relate in practical terms to understanding and performing popular music. In some cases, when there are several valid ways of explaining a certain idea, we have chosen to lessen confusion by limiting our explanation to the one approach we consider the most practical. This doesn't mean that other approaches are wrong, but simply that too many possibilities presented too early stand in the way of your ability to clearly see the fundamentals. What this book does *not* attempt to do is to show you detailed methods for improvising, arranging, or composing. While those subjects are referred to from time to time, the emphasis here is on understanding the basic principles of music so that you can begin to read, study and listen as an educated musician.

Since this book is written by players for players, we consider it to be essential that you also play what you see in this book. Only by getting these ideas off the page, onto an instrument (preferably keyboard or guitar, so that you can play the chords), and into your ear will you gain the full practical benefit. You don't need to have much technique, only the willingness to take the time to figure out the notes so that you can hear what's being described in words. Many times, a complicated idea will quickly make sense when you hear it connected to a familiar sound.

When you've finished this book, look back at that chart again, and you'll see how everything on the page now tells a story. You will have begun to understand a language that expresses things no other language can, and as a knowledgeable musician, you too will now be part of the conversation.

Carl Schroeder
Keith Wyatt

Part I: Tools
Notes, Rhythms, and Scales

No matter what the style or complexity, music can be most simply described as organized sound, and the purpose of studying harmony and theory is to learn the methods by which sounds are organized in both large and small ways. The first step in this study is to learn the written language by which music is communicated from one musician to another. The system of musical notation we use now has been developed over hundreds of years and, like any language, continues to evolve. The capacity of these symbols to pass along both the broad and subtle elements of music are what allow a Chinese musician, for example, to perform a piece of music today just as a German composer intended it 300 years ago, or a guitar player to write a chart this afternoon and hear the band play it tonight.

It is very important that you develop a clear, consistent way of writing the various notes and rests so that other musicians will understand what you're saying. This involves a fair amount of repetition—simply drawing the symbols over and over until they become natural to your hand. In the process, their meaning will become clearer, so that you can think less about them as shapes and concentrate more on the music that comes from them. At the same time, it is very helpful if you study music reading on your instrument. By using notation in a practical way, you'll quickly get past the merely visual part and get to the music itself. As with any language, it only becomes usable through constant application.

Pitch

1

Music is made up of sounds that that can be organized into three main elements: *melody*, *rhythm*, and *harmony*. These elements are passed from one musician to another by *music notation*, which allows a reader to precisely locate and reproduce any musical sound by means of a set of symbols that represent both the *pitch* of a note (relative sense of high or low) and its *rhythm* (placement in time). We will look first at the symbols that represent *pitch*.

The system for representing pitch is based on assigning a different name to each note. These note names are the same as the first seven letters of the alphabet (A, B, C, D, E, F, and G) and together are called the *musical alphabet*. In spite of the large number of notes that can be produced by musical instruments, only seven note names are needed because the eighth note, called the *octave*, has the same sound as the first, but higher in pitch—and therefore uses the same letter name as the first note. The octave is both the end of the first set of notes and the beginning of the next. Different instruments are capable of producing sounds in different ranges of pitch, some in many different octaves and some in only a few, but all of these pitches are notated with the same seven letter names.

Fig. 1: the musical alphabet

A	B	C	D	E	F	G	A	B	C	D	etc.
1	2	3	4	5	6	7	8/1	2	3	4	
							octave				

To provide a consistent way of measuring pitch, notes are placed on a grid of five lines and four spaces called the *staff*. The lines and spaces are numbered from low to high to aid in showing the particular location of a note. The higher the pitch, the higher the note is placed on the staff.

Fig. 2: the staff

5 lines   4 spaces

Because different instruments produce higher or lower ranges of pitch, the staff can be made to represent different ranges of pitch by means of a *clef sign*. The two most common clef signs are *treble clef*, which is used to notate higher-pitched sounds (e.g., the guitar, the right hand of the keyboard), and *bass clef*, which is used to notate lower-pitched sounds (e.g., the bass, the left hand of the keyboard). These symbols, while universally recognized by their shape alone, are carefully placed on the staff so that they draw attention to specific notes.

The treble clef (also called the "G clef") spirals around the line where the note "G" is located.

Fig. 3: the treble clef

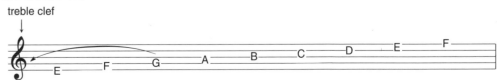

The treble clef is drawn in two parts, with each part drawn from top to bottom, as shown below. Draw a line of treble clefs, being careful to end each spiral on the second line, and to keep the shape clear and simple.

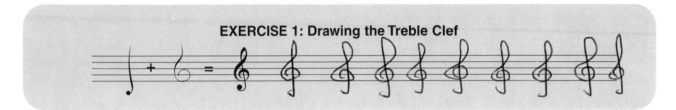

EXERCISE 1: Drawing the Treble Clef

The bass clef (also called the "F clef") has dots on either side of the line where the note "F" is found.

Fig. 4: the bass clef

The bass clef is drawn as shown; center the dot at the end of the spiral on the fourth line along with the two separate dots. Draw a line of bass clefs.

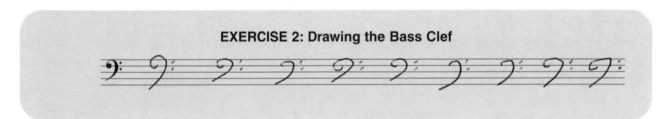

EXERCISE 2: Drawing the Bass Clef

Because the keyboard uses both the treble and bass clef, the two are placed one above the other and joined together to form the *grand staff*. This way, both the highest and lowest pitches can be seen and played together. The note that falls between the two clefs is called *middle C;* as it belongs to neither clef, it is drawn with a short line of its own.

Fig. 5: the grand staff

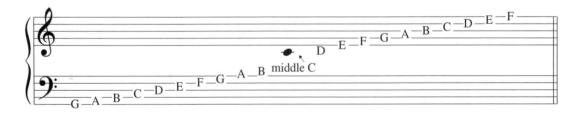

Ever since the modern staff was developed, various methods have been used to help beginners memorize the names of the notes. One of the most traditional and effective methods is to memorize sentences in which the first letter of each word represents the notes in ascending order on either the lines or the spaces of the treble or bass clefs. Here are the classic sentences used by generations of English-speaking music students:

Treble clef lines (in order from low to high):	E	G	B	D	F
The sentence is:	Every	Good	Boy	Does	Fine
Treble clef spaces:	F	A	C	E	
Since the notes themselves spell the word "**FACE**," this is a good enough reminder as is.					
Bass clef lines:	G	B	D	F	A
The sentence is:	Good	Boys	Do	Fine	Always
Bass clef spaces:	A	C	E	G	
The sentence is:	All	Cows	Eat	Grass	

It has also been the traditional habit of music students to invent their own versions of these memory-prompting devices using more personal sets of references. The more humorous or striking the image, the more likely that it will be accurately remembered. Feel free to improvise.

EXERCISE 3: Naming Notes on the Staff

Name the notes written on the staff. Write the letter name of each note in the space provided.

EXERCISE 4: Drawing Notes on the Staff

Draw the indicated notes within the staff in all possible octaves. (The first one is done for you.)

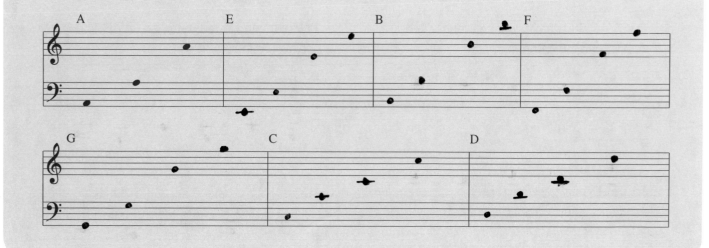

If a pitch extends beyond the range of either of the two clefs, this temporary extension is indicated by means of a short line (like that used to notate middle C), which is drawn through the note and called a *ledger line*. Ledger lines function like the lines of the staff, and notes can be placed between the lines just as in the spaces of a staff. Again, memorization is required; simply counting spaces and lines alphabetically up or down from the staff works at first, then with repetition the names become familiar.

Fig. 6: ledger lines

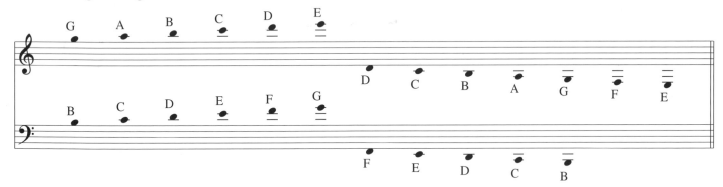

EXERCISE 5: Naming Notes on Ledger Lines

Name the notes on the ledger lines above and below the staff.

name: C   D   F   A   B   E   E   B   A   C   G

name: E   F   B   C   D   G   C   E   D

EXERCISE 6: Writing Notes on Ledger Lines

Write the indicated notes on ledger lines *above* the indicated clef.

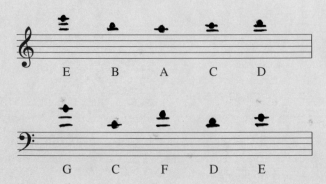

E   B   A   C   D

G   C   F   D   E

Write the indicated notes on ledger lines *below* the indicated clef.

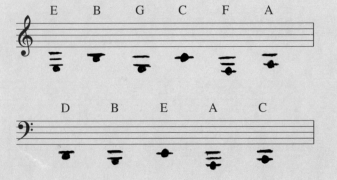

E   B   G   C   F   A

D   B   E   A   C

Major Scales
2 and Sharp Keys

ow that we have a system for arranging pitches on the staff using musical notation, we will look at how pitches are organized into groups.

Popular music, and almost all music anywhere in the world, is *tonal;* that is, its melodies and harmonies tend to be centered around a single musical pitch called a *tonic.* A group of pitches arranged in steps around a tonic is called a *scale,* and the scale that forms the basis of most melodies is the *major scale.* The major scale is also known as a *diatonic scale,* meaning that it contains all seven notes of the musical alphabet (called *scale degrees* or *steps*), arranged in a specific pattern above the tonic. The pattern, or formula, for the major scale is made up of an ascending series of *whole steps* (the equivalent of a two-fret span on a guitar or bass, or two keys on a keyboard) and *half steps* (the distance of one fret or one key). This formula never varies, regardless of the tonic on which it begins.

The formula for the major scale, showing the distance from each note of the scale to the next, is as follows:

Fig. 1: the formula for the major scale

(W = whole step, H = half step)

Notice that the half steps occur between the third and fourth degrees and the seventh and eighth degrees of the scale. This formula is the same regardless of the letter name of the tonic, or *key,* on which the scale is built, so the scale can be moved, or *transposed,* to any key and still have the same sound.

Applying the major scale formula to the key of C, the resulting scale looks like this:

Fig. 2: the C major scale

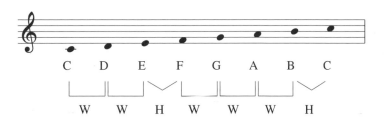

In C major, the half steps occur between the notes E–F and B–C. These are called *naturally occurring half steps,* because the distance between these notes is naturally a half step, while the distance between all of the other notes is naturally a whole step. You can easily see this on a keyboard because these pairs of notes have no black key between them. Since the key of C major can be played on the keyboard using only white keys, it is the easiest key to see and play on that instrument.

If a major scale starts on a tonic other than C, the major scale formula will require that modifications be made to the notes of the musical alphabet. To see why this is, begin a major scale on the tonic G, and build the scale step by step according to the formula (W-W-H-W-W-W-H):

EXERCISE 1

Build a G major scale on the staff below.

The formula states that there must be a whole step between the sixth and seventh degrees, and a half step between the seventh degree and the octave, but the naturally occurring half step between E and F causes a mismatch. The solution is to raise the seventh degree, F, by a half step in pitch, thereby increasing its distance from E and decreasing its distance from G, the octave. This is accomplished by using a *sharp sign (#)* in front of the F. A sharp sign has the effect of raising the following note one half step in pitch.

Fig. 3: the sharp sign

When F is raised to F♯, the G scale fits the major scale formula. This means that a G major scale must always contain an F♯.

NOTE: When spoken, the sharp is said after the name of the note, as in "F sharp." Likewise, when written in text, the sharp follows the letter name: F♯. When written as a note on the staff, however, the sharp is always written before the note, centered on exactly the same line or space as the note itself.

EXERCISE 2

Write a sharp before each of the notes shown on the staff. Place the sharp slightly to the left of the note, centered on the same line or space, with the horizontal lines angled slightly up, as shown:

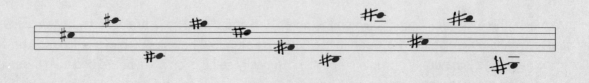

EXERCISE 3

Each of the following major keys requires the use of sharps. Build the scales according to the formula, adding the sharps where necessary.

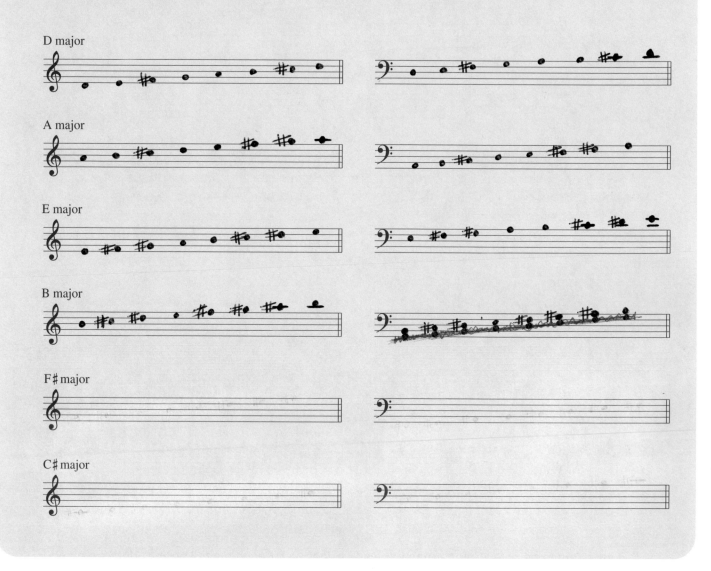

Because each of these scales always requires the use of one or more sharps in its construction, for convenience, the sharps are collected at the beginning of a piece of music next to the clef sign. This is called the *key signature*. Placing the key signature at the beginning indicates that the sharps are to be automatically applied throughout the piece in all octaves. (This saves the time that would otherwise be spent writing the sharps in front of each individual note.) Sharps in a key signature are written on the staff in a specific octave and order, *which never varies*: F♯, C♯, G♯, D♯, A♯, E♯, and B♯.

Fig. 4: the order of sharps in a key signature

The key signature of C♯ major contains all seven sharps. All other sharp key signatures have fewer. For each sharp key signature, draw the necessary number of sharps starting with F♯ and continuing, in order, to the right.

EXERCISE 4

Write the key signatures for each of the sharp keys next to the clef signs.

It is important to be able to *quickly* name the key signature for each major key, including the number and order of sharps. To help memorize the key signatures of sharp keys, use this system:

1. Memorize these letters in order, forward and backward:

    B   E   A   D   -   G   C   F

2. To name the key signature of a sharp key, count from *right to left* until you arrive at the letter name *one step in pitch below the tonic of the key*. This gives you the number and order of sharps in the key. For example:

    Question: What is the key signature of E major?
    Answer: D is the note one step in pitch below E. Counting the letters of the formula
                  from right to left, D is the fourth letter. Therefore, the key signature of E
                  major contains four sharps. In order, they are F♯, C♯, G♯, and D♯.

EXERCISE 5

Complete the exercise by naming the number and names of the sharps each key contains:

Key	Number of sharps	Names of sharps (in order)
D major	_____	_____
A major	_____	_____
E major	_____	_____
B major	_____	_____
F♯ major	_____	_____
C♯ major	_____	_____

It is equally important to be able to look at a key signature on the staff and instantly name the key. When looking at a sharp key signature on the staff, the tonic of the key is the note one half step above the last sharp to the right.

Looking at the key signature below, the last sharp to the right is A♯. One half step above that note is B; therefore, the key signature is B major.

Fig. 5: recognizing sharp key signatures

EXERCISE 6

Name the keys represented by the following key signatures:

key: _____   _____   _____   _____

_____   _____   _____   _____

Flat Keys and Accidentals

3

As we have seen, major scales in certain keys require the use of sharps in order to match the notes of the musical alphabet to the major scale formula. There are still other keys that must be modified in another way to fit the formula. To see why this is, begin a major scale on the tonic F, and build the scale step by step according to the formula (add a clef sign):

EXERCISE 1: The F Major Scale

Build an F major scale on the staff below.

The formula requires that there be a half step between the third and fourth scale degrees and a whole step between the fourth and fifth, but the naturally occurring half step between B and C causes a mismatch. The solution is to lower the fourth degree, B, by a half step in pitch, thereby decreasing its distance from A and increasing its distance from C. This is accomplished by using a *flat sign (♭)* in front of the B. A flat sign has the effect of lowering the following note one half step in pitch.

Fig. 1: the flat sign

When B is lowered to B♭, the F scale fits the major scale formula. This means that the F major scale must always contain a B♭.

NOTE: Like sharps, the flat is spoken after the name of the note but written on the staff before the note, centered on exactly the same line or space as the note itself.

EXERCISE 2

Write a flat before each of the notes shown on the staff. Place the flat slightly to the left of the note, with the open part centered on the same line or space as the notehead, as shown.

EXERCISE 3

Each of the following major keys requires the use of flats. Build the scales according to the formula, adding the flats where necessary. Key signatures contain either sharps *or* flats, never both.

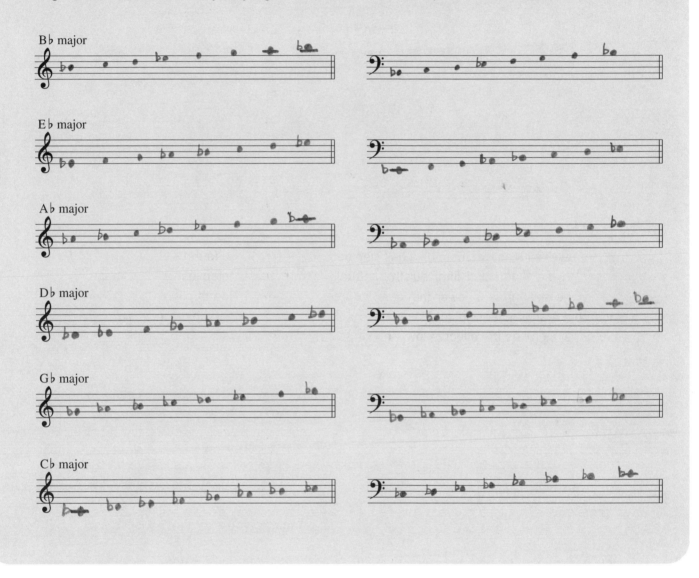

Like the sharps, the flats are collected at the beginning of any piece of music in a flat key to form the key signature. Flat key signatures are written in a specific order and octave that *does not vary.*

Fig. 2: the order of flats in a key signature

If less than seven flats are required for the key signature, draw the necessary number starting with the B♭ and continuing to the right.

EXERCISE 4

Write the key signatures for each of the flat keys next to the clef signs as described above.

It is important to be able to *quickly* name the key signature for each flat key, including the number and order of flats. To help memorize the key signatures of flat keys, use this system:

1. Use the same formula that was memorized for sharp keys:

B   E   A   D - G   C   F

2. To name the key signature of a flat key, count from *left to right* until you arrive at the letter name of the key, then go *one more letter to the right*. This gives you the number and order of flats in the key. For example:

Question:	What is the key signature of A♭ major?
Answer:	Counting from left to right, A is the third letter; the next letter to the right is D. Therefore, the key of A♭ contains four flats. In order, they are B♭, E♭, A♭, and D♭.

Chapter 3

It is equally important that you be able to look at a key signature on the staff and instantly name the key. When looking at a flat key signature on the staff, the tonic of the key is the same as the *second flat from the right*. Looking at the key signature below, for instance, the second flat from the right is D♭; therefore, the key is D♭.

Fig. 3: recognizing flat key signatures

NOTE: When someone is speaking the name of a key, to know right away whether it is a sharp key or flat key, remember that all flat keys, except the key of F, have the word "flat" in their name, such as B-flat, E-flat, A-flat, etc.

Enharmonics and Accidentals

If you count the number of flat keys (seven), the number of sharp keys (seven), and add the key of C, the total number of keys is fifteen, yet there are only twelve half steps in an octave. The reason for this apparent contradiction is that some pitches have two names—specifically, D♭ and C♯, G♭ and F♯, C♭ and B. When a pitch has two possible names, their relationship is described as *enharmonic*. Enharmonic tones sound the same but are spelled differently. Depending on the nature of the instrument and the context of the melody or harmony, one of the two possible names usually emerges as the best choice in a given situation.

EXERCISE 5

Write the C♯ major and D♭ major scales on the staff, and compare them note for note. Are the two scales enharmonic? _YES_

C♯ major   D♭ major

EXERCISE 6

Write the enharmonic equivalent next to each of the notes below. Remember the naturally occurring half steps; these will affect some of your answers. (Watch the clef sign!)

Sharps and flats may also be used outside of a key signature to temporarily change the pitch of a note to suit a particular melody or harmony. When this happens, the sharps or flats are called *accidentals*. A third type of accidental exists, which cancels a previously applied sharp or flat; it is called a *natural sign*. Natural signs, like sharps and flats, are drawn slightly to the left and directly in front of the note.

Fig. 4: the natural sign

B-flat   B-natural

EXERCISE 7

Draw a natural sign before each of the notes on the staff. Place the natural sign to the left of the note, with the open part centered on the same line or space, and with the horizontal lines angled slightly up, as shown.

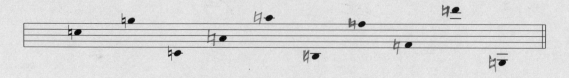

Intervals

4

A scale is a pattern of notes centered around a tonic. Within that overall pattern are smaller patterns, right down to the relationships between individual notes that form the building blocks of both melodies and harmonies. By knowing these small relationships, it is easier to gain a much greater understanding of the larger patterns and to learn to control the emotional effects they create in listeners.

Interval Quantity

The distance between any two musical tones is described as an *interval.* If the tones are played one after the other, as in a melody, they form a *melodic interval.* The names of the intervals are based on the number of scale tones they contain. For example, the distance from C to D contains two scale tones, that is, C and D; therefore it is a *second* interval. The distance from C to E contains three scale tones, C–D–E, so it is a *third* interval. Intervals are the same whether measured from the lower note or from the upper note; for instance, the distance from E *down* to C, containing three scale tones E–D–C, is still a third interval.

The number of scale tones an interval contains is called the *interval quantity.* The quantity is counted the same way in any key. For instance, the quantity of the interval B♭ up to E♭, containing four scale tones, B♭–C–D–E♭, is a *fourth* interval; the presence of flats does not alter the interval quantity. Likewise, the distance from C♯ to G♯ is a *fifth* interval, because it contains five scale tones, C♯–D♯–E♯–F♯–G♯, and the sharps do not affect the quantity. If the interval contains eight scale tones, it is called an *octave;* also, the distance between two notes of exactly the same pitch (containing *only one* scale tone) is called a *unison.*

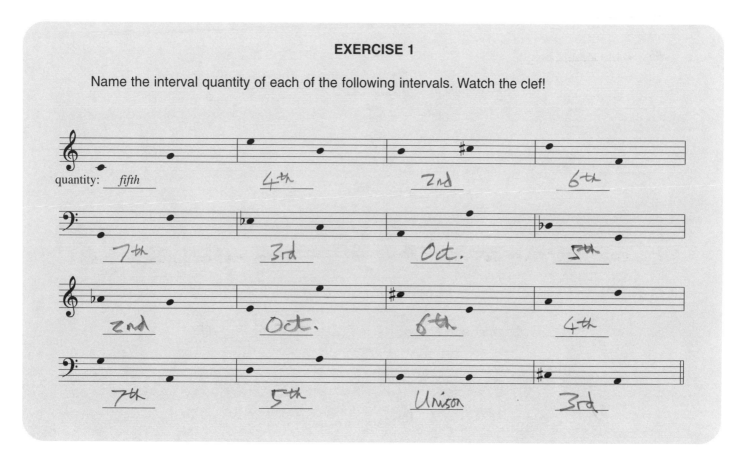

EXERCISE 1

Name the interval quantity of each of the following intervals. Watch the clef!

quantity: _fifth_   4th   2nd   6th

7th   3rd   Oct.   5th

2nd   Oct.   6th   4th

7th   5th   Unison   3rd

Interval Quality

Some intervals contain the same number of scale tones, yet still look and sound different.

Fig. 1

Although both intervals above contain three scale tones, the exact distance from C to E is different than that from C to E♭. Interval quantity gives us a general measurement of the size of the interval. The exact measurement is called the *interval quality*, which is the number of half steps the interval contains. Quality can be measured in comparison to the major scale.

How To Name Interval Quality

1. Determine the quantity by counting the scale tones.

2. If the upper note of the interval belongs to the major scale of the lower note, name it as follows:

major second

major third

perfect fourth

perfect fifth

major sixth

major seventh

perfect octave

3. If the upper note does not belong to the major scale of the lower note, name it as follows:

•If it is one half step smaller than a major interval, it is called *minor*.
•If it is one half step smaller than a perfect or minor interval, it is called *diminished*.
•If it is one half step larger than a perfect or major interval, it is called *augmented*.

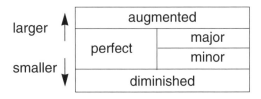

Fig. 2: interval qualities

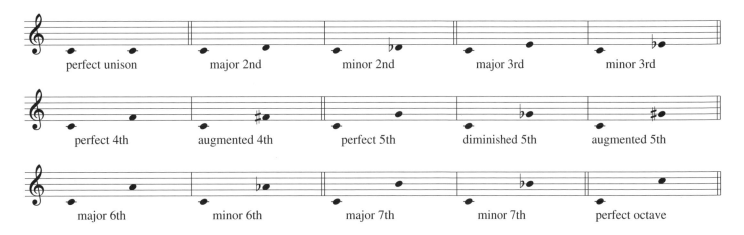

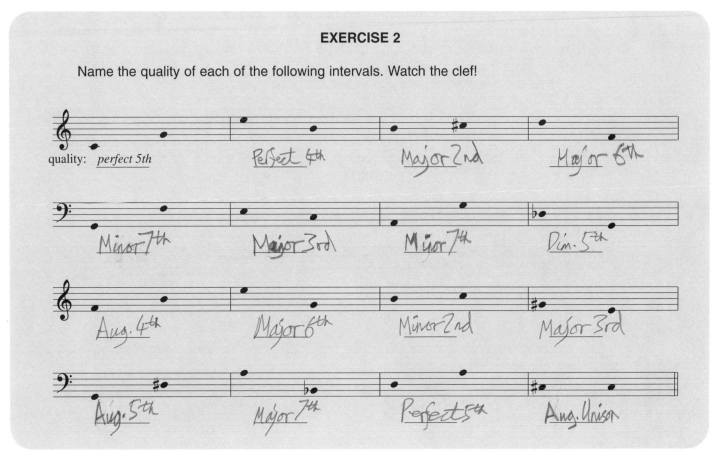

EXERCISE 2

Name the quality of each of the following intervals. Watch the clef!

quality: *perfect 5th*   Perfect 4th   Major 2nd   Major 6th

Major 7th   Major 3rd   Major 7th   Dim. 5th

Aug. 4th   Major 6th   Minor 2nd   Major 3rd

Aug. 5th   Major 7th   Perfect 5th   Aug. Unison

Building Intervals

To build a melodic interval going up, think of the given note as "1," and count the number of major scale tones indicated by the quantity. If the given interval is perfect or major, the process is complete. If not, adjust the major scale interval up or down to match the desired quality.

Fig. 3: building ascending melodic intervals

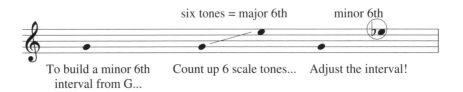

six tones = major 6th   minor 6th

To build a minor 6th   Count up 6 scale tones...   Adjust the interval!
interval from G...

NOTE: Raising a note does not always imply the use of a sharp, nor does lowering note always imply the use of a flat. The key signature of the lower note will determine which accidental, if any, is appropriate.

EXERCISE 3

Write the indicated intervals above the notes. Abbreviations for quality are as follows:

M for major   P for perfect   d for diminished
m for minor   A for augmented

To build descending melodic intervals, the bottom note must be raised or lowered to achieve the desired quality. Starting with the given note, count down the number of letter names indicated by the quantity. Now measure the distance from the lower note back to the upper. If the upper note belongs to the major scale of the lower note and the desired interval is perfect or major, the process is complete. If not, adjust the lower note up or down to achieve the proper quality.

Fig. 4: building descending melodic intervals

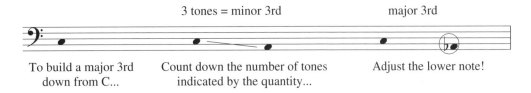

To build a major 3rd down from C... — Count down the number of tones indicated by the quantity... — Adjust the lower note!

EXERCISE 4

Write the indicated intervals below the notes.

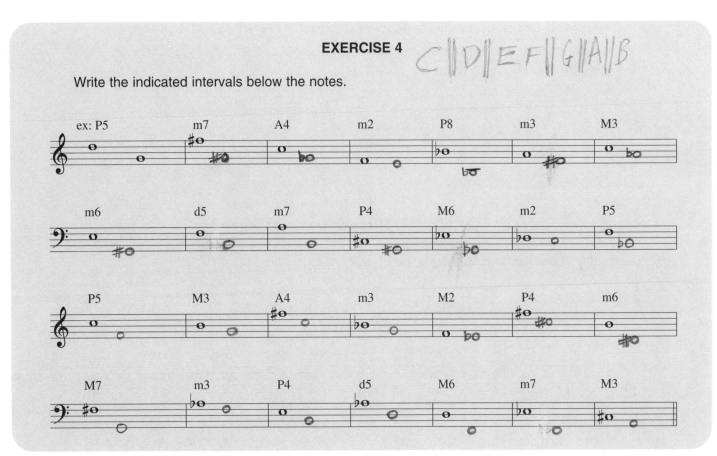

If two notes are played simultaneously, they form a *harmonic interval*. The quantity and quality of harmonic intervals is counted in exactly the same way as that of melodic intervals.

Fig. 5: melodic and harmonic intervals

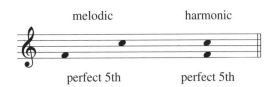

When augmented or diminished intervals are formed in certain keys, the presence of existing sharps or flats in the key signature plus the raised or lowered fifth interval can create a situation in which a pitch must be raised or lowered twice from its natural position. This is accomplished by means of accidentals called *double sharps* and *double flats*. The double sharp is formed by writing an "×" in front of the note.

Fig. 6: the double sharp

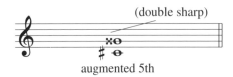

The double flat is formed by drawing two flats next to each other in front of the note.

Fig. 7: the double flat

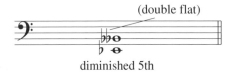

EXERCISE 5

Identify the following intervals using these abbreviations to name the quality:

M for major   P for perfect   d for diminished
m for minor   A for augmented

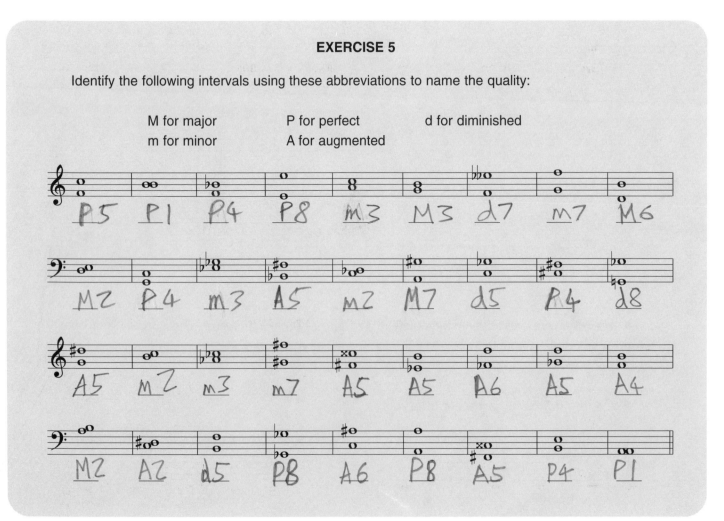

Triads

5

    A melodic interval—two notes, one after the other—is the smallest unit of melody. Likewise, a harmonic interval—two notes played together—is the smallest unit of harmony. It takes two or more tones written or played simultaneously to form a *chord*. Most basic chords are made up of specific arrangements of *three* notes, and these are called *triads*. Understanding how to build and identify the four types of triads is the first step toward understanding more complex chords and the progressions that are created when chords are put together.

    The first note of a triad, which gives the triad its name, is the *root.* The root has the same relationship to a triad as the tonic has to a scale; it is the fundamental note. In addition to the root, a triad contains the note a third interval above the root, called the *third,* and the note a fifth interval above the root, called the *fifth.*

Fig. 1: C triad

    There are two types of triads that are extremely common: *major triads* and *minor triads*. Their popularity is due to the fact that they are both *consonant;* that is, they have a sound that is generally described as smooth, stable, or restful. Although both triad types contain a root, third, and fifth, their thirds have different qualities, which gives them their distinct sounds. The quality of the third in the major triad is a *major third*, and the quality of the third in the minor triad is a *minor third*. Both triads contain a perfect fifth. When written on chord charts, the letter name of the chord by itself is the symbol for a major triad—the letter "C," for instance, is the symbol for "C major"—while the minor triad is symbolized by the letter name followed by "mi," as in "Cmi." Like interval qualities, the differences in triads are called *triad qualities.*

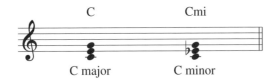

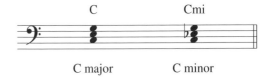

EXERCISE 1

    Name the quality, major or minor, of each of these triads. Use the letter name of the root for major triads and the letter name plus "mi" for minor triads.

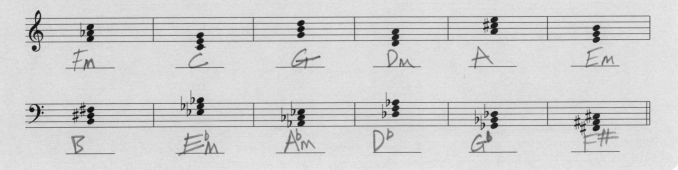

EXERCISE 2

Build major triads above the following roots.

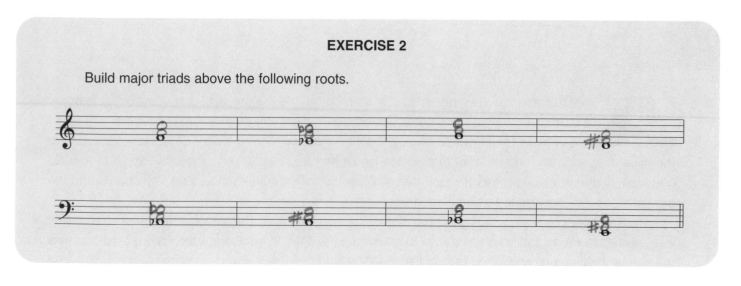

EXERCISE 3

Build minor triads above the following roots.

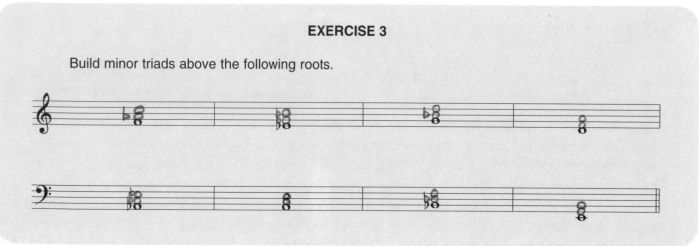

In addition to major and minor triads, there are two other types of triad qualities. One is a triad containing a root, major third, and augmented fifth; this is called an *augmented triad*. In the chord symbol for the augmented triad, the quality is symbolized by "+" as in "C+." The other triad quality contains a root, minor third, and diminished fifth and is called a *diminished triad*. Its quality is symbolized by " ° " as in "C°." Augmented and diminished triads are considered *dissonant*—tense, or even jarring. These triads are used in chord progressions in ways that will be described later in this book.

Fig. 3: C augmented and C diminished

Chapter 5

EXERCISE 4

Name the quality, augmented or diminished, of each of these triads. Use the appropriate chord symbols.

G+   F°   A♭+   F#+

C#+   A♭°   F+   B°

EXERCISE 5

Build augmented triads on each of the following roots.

EXERCISE 6

Build diminished triads on each of the following roots.

EXERCISE 7

Build the appropriate triads on the indicated roots.

B+   A♭   Ami   B♭mi   G+

D♭mi   E   E♭°   D   F°

Note Values

6

So far, we have explored two of the three main elements of music: melody and harmony. Both of these elements involve arranging notes according to various patterns and formulas to form scales and chords. In order to actually perform a piece of music, however, it is also essential to arrange these notes in the context of time; that is, it is necessary to know when and for how long to play them. This brings us to the topic of *rhythm*—or, how pitches are placed in time.

Beats and Meter

Ordinary clock time is divided into various units of measure, of which the smallest is one second. Musical time is also divided into units of measure, of which the smallest is the *beat*—the underlying, regular rhythm of a piece of music. Just as seconds are grouped into minutes, repetitive patterns of strong (accented) and weak (unaccented) beats form the *meter*, or overall rhythmic feeling, of a piece of music. The meter usually consists of groups of 2, 3, or 4 beats, with the first beat of each group being the strongest, and this pattern usually stays the same throughout a piece of music in order to provide a consistent backdrop for the melody and harmony.

To notate rhythms on the staff, groups of beats are set apart from each other by vertical lines, called *bar lines*, drawn in front of the first beat of each group. The spaces between the lines are called *measures*, or *bars*.

Fig. 1: bar lines and measures

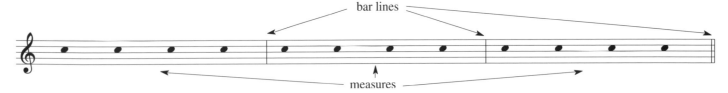

Within the context of the meter, the duration of each individual pitch is indicated by means of two sets of symbols: symbols for sound *(notes)* and symbols for silence *(rests)*. The durations of notes and rests are most easily understood in relation to the most common metric grouping, four beats in a measure.

A note that occupies a whole measure of four beats is called a *whole note*. It looks like an empty oval resting on its side. Its equivalent rest is the *whole rest*, which is suspended from the fourth line of the staff.

Fig. 2: whole note and whole rest

EXERCISE 1

Practice drawing whole notes and rests.

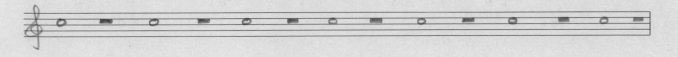

A note that lasts for half of a measure, or two beats, is called a *half note*. The half note resembles a whole note but with the addition of a *stem* attached to the *notehead*. If the pitch of the note is on the middle line of the staff or above, the stem is attached to the left side of the notehead, pointing down. If the pitch of the note is below the middle line, the stem is attached to the right side of the notehead, pointing up. The equivalent rest, the *half rest*, sits on the third line of the staff.

Fig. 3: half notes and rests

EXERCISE 2

Practice drawing half notes and half rests.

A note that lasts for one fourth of a measure, or one beat, is called a *quarter note*. The quarter note looks like a filled-in half note. The equivalent rest, the *quarter rest*, is drawn as shown.

Fig. 4: quarter notes and rests

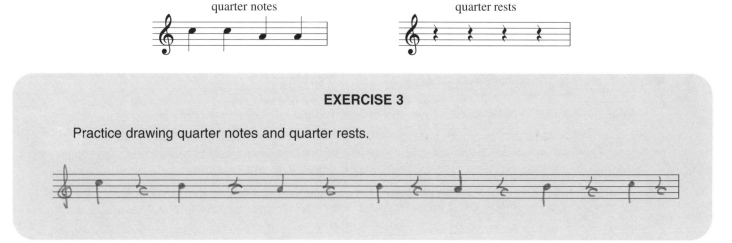

EXERCISE 3

Practice drawing quarter notes and quarter rests.

Divisions of the Beat

Just as seconds in ordinary time may be divided into fractions for more precise measurement of, say, a footrace, beats may also be divided into smaller units of musical time to accurately represent rhythms smaller than the quarter note.

A note that lasts for one half of a beat is called an *eighth note*. (Notice that it is also one eighth of a measure.) The eighth note is the same as a quarter note but with a *flag* attached to the stem, which is *always on the right side regardless of stem direction*. Generally, when two, three, or four eighth notes occur next to one another, they are connected together by means of a *beam*, which reduces the clutter of separate flags. The equivalent rest, the *eighth rest*, also has a single flag, which is drawn in the third space as shown. (Eighth rests are not beamed—as a rule, use a single larger rest rather than a group of small rests.)

Fig. 5: eighth notes and rests

EXERCISE 4

Practice drawing separate eighth notes, beamed eighth notes, and eighth rests.

The smallest common note value lasts for one fourth of a beat and is called a *sixteenth note*. It is the same as an eighth note but with two flags attached. When two or more sixteenth notes occur within a single beat, they are connected by a double beam. The equivalent rest, the *sixteenth rest,* also has two flags, which are drawn in the second and third spaces of the staff.

Fig. 6: sixteenth notes and rests

EXERCISE 5

Practice drawing separate sixteenth notes, beamed sixteenth notes, and rests.

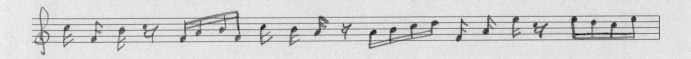

Eighth and sixteenth notes may be beamed together with each other by the use of *partial beams.* Partial beams *always point inward, never outward.*

Fig. 7: partial beams

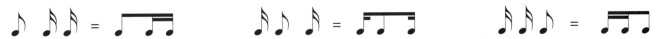

EXERCISE 6

Redraw the notes on the left side of the dash into one group by means of full or partial beams.

Beams should group notes so that individual beats can be clearly seen. When sixteenth notes are involved, each beat should be beamed separately from the others.

Fig. 8: beaming for clarity

When the melody moves up or down within a group of notes, follow the general direction of the notes by angling the beam up or down.

Fig. 9: beam angle

When beaming ledger lines, stems must be long enough so that all beams are within the staff.

Fig. 10: beaming with ledger lines

good   bad

EXERCISE 7

How many of the notes or rests on the right side of the equal sign does it take to equal the value of the note or rest on the left?

o = 4 ♩   ▬ = 2 ▬   𝅗𝅥 = 4 ♪   ▬ = 4 𝄾

𝄽 = 4 𝄾   o = 2 𝅗𝅥   𝅗𝅥 = 2 ♩   ▬ = 8 𝄾

EXERCISE 8

What single large note do these smaller note values add up to?

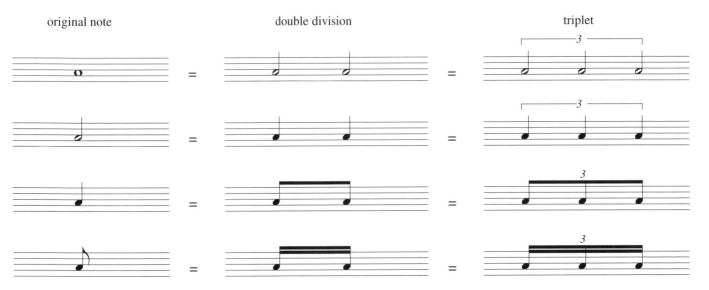

Triplets

When a note is divided into three equal parts instead of two, the result is called a *triplet*. A triplet occupies the same length of time normally occupied by two notes of the same value. This is indicated by drawing the number "3" above the group of notes and—if it is a quarter-note triplet, half-note triplet, or partial triplet of any kind—framing it with a square bracket.

Fig. 11: triplets

original note   double division   triplet

Rests and notes of the same value may be used in any combination within a triplet.

Fig. 12: triplets with rests

Dotted Notes

Placed immediately after and parallel to a notehead or rest, a *dot* increases the value of the note or rest by one half its normal duration. This makes it possible to create note values in between the normal notes without inventing a new type of notation.

Fig. 13: dotted notes and rests

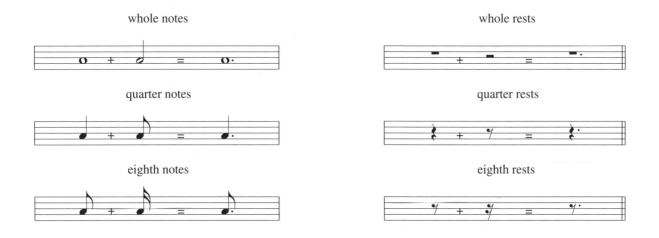

NOTE: The dotted whole rest is theoretically the equivalent of a dotted whole note, but in practice a simple whole rest is often used to indicate the total duration of a measure, regardless of how many beats there are in the measure.

EXERCISE 9

Draw the single dotted note or rest that is equivalent to the notes or rests on the left side of the equal sign.

EXERCISE 10

What single large note do these smaller notes add up to?

Spacing and Clarity

When writing music, it is very important to be extremely clear and organized so that a musician reading the notes can understand what is intended. Clarity in writing is essentially a matter of common sense; that is, the music should *look* the way it *sounds.*

Comparing all of the note values, one can see that each smaller note value divides the previous note value in two, so that two half notes or rests occupy the same amount of time as one whole note or rest, two quarter notes or rests occupy the same amount of time as one half note or rest, and so on. The same relationship is used when writing note values on the staff, so that a half note occupies twice the *space* of a quarter note, etc. This keeps the appearance of the music in proportion to the way it sounds, and makes it much easier for a reader to interpret the music properly the first time.

Fig. 14: proportionate spacing of note values

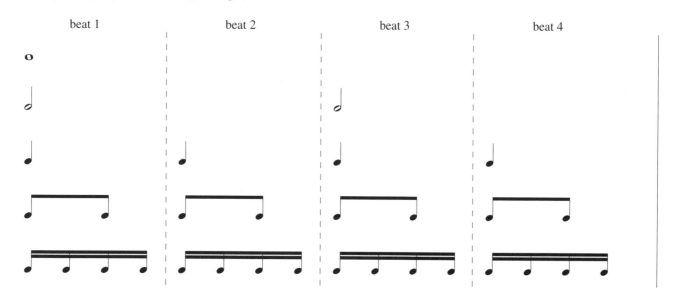

EXERCISE 11

The following example uses incorrect spacing, stems, and beams. Rewrite the example on the staff provided using correct notation.

Time Signatures and Ties

7

As explained in Chapter 6, *meter* is the grouping of beats into repetitive patterns. These patterns are generally made up of groups of two, three, or four beats. Technically, this description of beat patterns seems rather dry and mathematical, but in fact these patterns are essentially a way to notate various dance rhythms that have been popular at one time or another, which are then labeled as musical styles. For example, here are the common beat patterns along with the dance styles they typically represent. The accompanying words illustrate how the beat patterns are accented:

Fig. 1: meter and style

Groups of 2: march, polka, samba, country music

Accent pattern

| *AP* | - | ple | | *AP* | - | ple |
| *STRONG* | - | weak | | *STRONG* | - | weak |

Groups of 3: waltzes (Viennese waltz, jazz waltz, country waltz)

Accent pattern

| *BLUE* | - | ber | - | ry | | *BLUE* | - | ber | - | ry |
| *STRONG* | - | weak | - | weak | | *STRONG* | - | weak | - | weak |

Groups of 4: most other popular styles, including rock, funk, jazz, blues, disco, etc.

Accent pattern

| *HOT* | - | po | - | ta | - | to | | *HOT* | - | po | - | ta | - | to |
| *STRONG* | - | weak | - | *weak** | - | weak | | *STRONG* | - | weak | - | *weak* | - | weak |

(*The third beat in a group of four generally receives an accent of its own.)

Time Signatures

The meter of a piece of music is indicated at the beginning, just to the right of the key signature, by a symbol called the *time signature*. This consists of two numbers, one above the other. The top number indicates how many beats there are in each measure, usually 4. The bottom number indicates which note value receives one beat, almost always the quarter note, also shown by the number 4. Thus, the most common time signature is 4/4, which is the basic meter of rock, funk, blues, and even most jazz and fusion. A time signature of 3/4 most commonly indicates a waltz, while 2/4 is found in some country music, some styles of Latin music, marches, and polkas.

Fig. 2: time signatures

In theory, any number, such as 7, could be used as the upper number, and any number representing a note value, such as 8 (for the eighth note), could be used as the lower number. Time signatures of this type do occur from time to time in more complex styles of music, but they are far less common than those described above. The time signature of 4/4, in fact, is so common that it is also known as *common time*, symbolized by the letter "C" on the staff in place of the usual time signature.

Fig. 3: common time

A related time signature, in which the 4/4 time signature is cut in half, making it 2/2, is called *cut time*. This is symbolized by the letter "C" with a vertical line drawn through it.

Fig. 4: cut time

Regardless of which time signature is used, all beats of every measure must always be occupied fully by some combination of either notes or rests. The total value of all notes and rests in a measure may never be any more or less than the number indicated by the time signature.

EXERCISE 1

Add bar lines to each of the following examples to fit the time signatures.

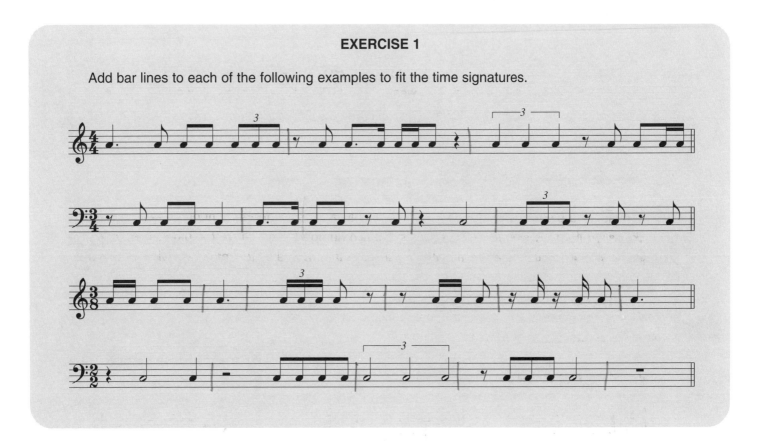

EXERCISE 2

Each measure in the example below contains less than the correct number of beats. Add the single note value that is necessary to make each measure complete.

EXERCISE 3

Add the one rest to each measure that will make it properly match the time signature.

EXERCISE 4

Rewrite each example on the following line to fit the new time signature. Change the value of each note or rest proportionately.

Ties

A *tie* is curved line that connects two notes of the same pitch for the purpose of combining their time value. Tied notes are treated the same as a single note, with the second note held as an extension of the first. When writing a tie, begin as close to the notehead as possible, and curve *away* from the stem of the note.

Ties are used in three places:

1. Across a barline

When the sound of a note sustains across a barline, a tie must be used to maintain the proper number of beats in each measure.

2. Across the middle of a measure with an even number of beats

When writing music, it is very important to keep the notes in the measure visually organized. By using a tie to sustain a note over the middle of the bar, rather than a single, longer note value, it is easier to see the division of the measure and therefore easier to read the music.

3. Across the beats of a measure when writing sixteenth notes or rests (or smaller values)

For the same reason that the middle of the bar is kept clear by use of the tie, each beat must visually stand alone when there are small note values, in order to avoid confusion.

Although at first glance they appear to be the same, a tie should not be confused with a *slur*, which is used to indicate the smooth phrasing of two or more notes of *different* pitch.

Fig. 5: slurs

EXERCISE 5

Rewrite the following examples using ties where necessary (according to the rules above) and beaming eighth and sixteenth notes that belong to the same beat.

Minor Scales

8

In the simplest terms, there are two primary emotional qualities in music: major and minor. The major quality, as heard in the major scale, is almost universally perceived as "bright" or "happy" and forms the basis of a large number of melodies in a great variety of styles. The minor quality, on the other hand, is usually perceived as "dark" or "sad," a quality reflected in *minor scales.* There are several different versions of minor scales, but the essential difference between the major and minor qualities comes down to a single note: the third scale degree. The major scale has a *major third* degree, while all minor scales have a *minor third* degree. This small difference in interval quality, and its resulting emotional effect, is one of the most powerful in music.

The Natural Minor Scale

Like the major scale, the natural minor scale is made up of a series of whole steps and half steps arranged in a particular order. The interval formula for the natural minor scale is as follows:

Fig. 1: the formula for the natural minor scale

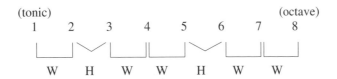

Notice that in this formula, the half steps are between the *second and third* and the *fifth and sixth* degrees. Applying this formula from the tonic note A, the scale looks like this:

Fig. 2: the A natural minor scale

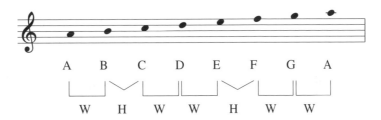

The naturally occurring half steps between B–C and E–F fall in exactly the right place to fit the scale formula, which means that the A natural minor scale requires no sharps or flats in its construction.

Because natural minor scales are the basic diatonic scales of the minor quality, they are considered *minor keys* and have their own key signatures, just like major keys. Therefore, the key of A minor has a key signature of *no sharps and no flats.*

The rules for building other minor scales and key signatures are the same as for major keys: from the tonic, write the letter names of the notes in order, apply the interval formula, and adjust scale tones up or down by means of sharps or flats as needed.

EXERCISE 1

Build an E natural minor scale on the staves.

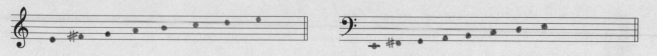

The natural minor formula states that there must be a whole step between the tonic and second degrees and a half step between the second and third, but, in Exercise 1 above, the naturally occurring half step between E and F causes a mismatch. The solution is to raise the second degree, F, a half step in pitch by means of a sharp sign, thereby increasing its distance from E and decreasing its distance from G. If you haven't done so already, add the sharp sign to the F in the exercise above. The scale now fits the formula, which means that the E natural minor scale must always contain an F♯. To form the key signature for E minor, place the F♯ on the staff next to the clef sign.

Now build a natural minor scale from the tonic D, following the formula:

EXERCISE 2

Build a D natural minor scale on the staves.

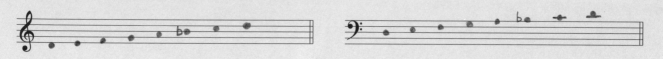

The formula states that there must be a half step between the fifth and sixth degrees and a whole step between the seventh degree and the octave, but the naturally occurring half step between B and C causes a mismatch. The solution is to lower the seventh degree, B, a half step in pitch by means of a flat sign, thereby decreasing its distance from A and increasing its distance from C. If you haven't done so already, add the flat sign to the B in Exercise 2. The scale now fits the formula, which means that the D natural minor scale must always contain a B♭. Place the Bb on the staff next to the clef sign if you want to form the key signature.

EXERCISE 3

Build the natural minor scales in each of the keys below. Write in the accidentals as they occur; these scales require the use of sharps only.

EXERCISE 3 (cont'd)

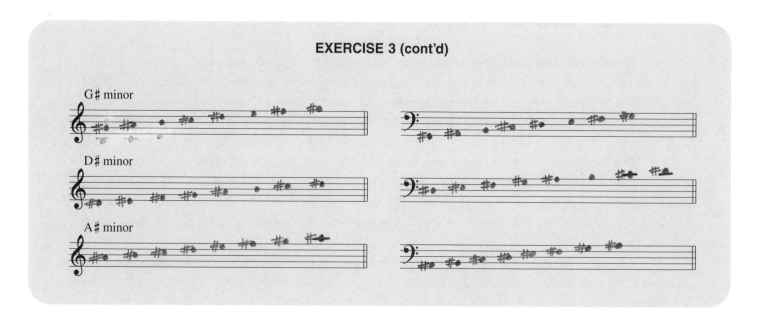

G# minor

D# minor

A# minor

EXERCISE 4

Build the natural minor scales in each of the keys below. Write in the accidentals as they occur; these scales require the use of flats only.

G minor

C minor

F minor

B♭ minor

E♭ minor

A♭ minor

Relative Minor Keys

In the process of developing the natural minor scales and key signatures, you may have noticed that the use of sharps and flats results in key signatures that resemble those we have already seen. That is, the absence of sharps or flats from the key signature of A minor makes it look like the key signature of C major; E minor, with one sharp, looks like G major; and D minor, with one flat, looks like F major. Major and minor keys that are built on different tonic notes but share the same key signatures are described as *relative keys*. For each major key, there is a *relative minor*, and for each minor key, a *relative major*. To the eye, the key signatures of relative keys are identical. Minor key signatures are laid out on the staff just like major key signatures. The sharps and flats are in the same octave and same order, *which never varies*. Only by analyzing the melody to locate the tonic can a key signature be identified as major or minor.

The distance from the tonic of a major key to the tonic of its relative minor is always *down a minor third*—e.g., C down to A, G down to E, and F down to D. To help remember this relationship, think of minor as feeling "down," then count down three scale degrees from the tonic of the major scale. Notice also that the tonic of the relative minor is the same note as the *sixth degree* of the relative major. Using this knowledge, it is possible to find the key signatures of minor keys without actually writing the scales out.

EXERCISE 5

For every major key listed, find the relative minor, and write its key signature on the staff. The first three are done for you.

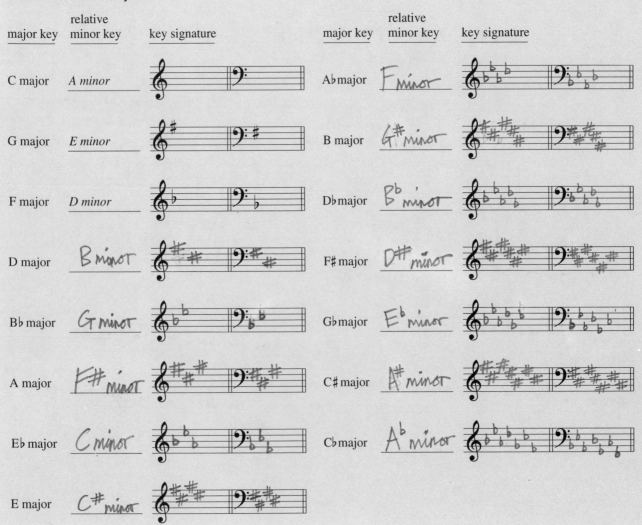

Another way to find minor key signatures quickly is by counting *up a minor third* from the tonic of the minor key to the tonic of its relative major—e.g., from A up to C, E up to G, and D up to F. Think of major as being an "up" feeling, then count up three scale degrees from the tonic of the minor key. Notice that the tonic of the relative major key is the same note as the *third degree* of the minor key. Once you find the tonic of the relative major, you can then name the key signature for both major and relative minor.

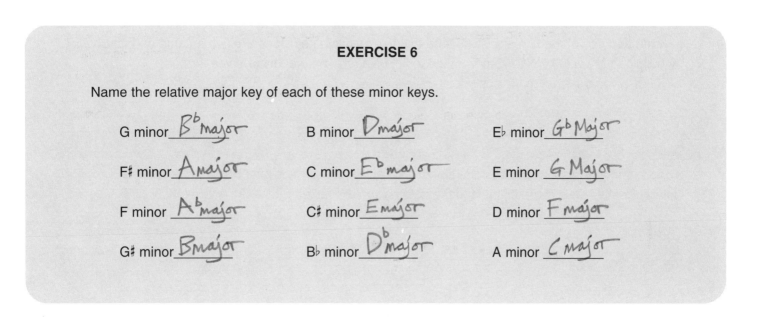

EXERCISE 6

Name the relative major key of each of these minor keys.

G minor _Bb major_   B minor _D major_   Eb minor _Gb Major_

F# minor _A Major_   C minor _Eb major_   E minor _G Major_

F minor _Ab major_   C# minor _E Major_   D minor _F major_

G# minor _B Major_   Bb minor _Db major_   A minor _C Major_

Parallel Minor Keys

There is another relationship between major and minor keys that is also useful in comparing scale structure and key signatures. This is the relationship between *parallel major and minor keys*. Parallel keys are those that are built on the same tonic but have different key signatures, for example, C major and C minor. The parallel relationship offers a step-by-step comparison of the construction of the two scales.

EXERCISE 7

On the first staff, build one octave of the C major scale. On the staff below it, build the C natural minor scale. Add accidentals next to the notes where necessary.

Comparing the two scales visually, it is obvious that three notes in the C minor scale are different than those in the C major scale. If the scale steps are numbered, they compare as follows:

C major: 1   2   3   4   5   6   7   8

C minor: 1   2   ♭3   4   5   ♭6   ♭7   8

Based on this comparison, it is clear that the C minor scale can be built by lowering the third, sixth, and seventh degrees of the C major scale, and that the resulting key signature is the same as that obtained by building the scale step by step from the tonic, using the natural minor scale formula.

Now compare the A major scale to its parallel minor:

EXERCISE 8

On the first staff, build one octave of the A major scale. On the staff below it, build the A natural minor scale. Add accidentals next to the notes where necessary.

A major

A minor

Comparing the two scales, the A minor scale looks like an A major scale without the sharps—that is, the third, sixth, and seventh degrees have been lowered, just as when comparing C major and C minor, but this time by eliminating a sharp rather than by adding a flat. The resulting key signature for A minor, no sharps or flats, is again the same as that obtained by using the formula to build the scale from its tonic.

The comparison of parallel major and minor scales is the same for every key and results in a simple and very common way to describe the natural minor scale: *as a major scale with a lowered third, sixth, and seventh.* This view is accurate and provides a handy way to quickly compare the scales. Remember, however, that this comparison is only technical. The different emotional quality of natural minor scales results from a structure that is very different from major scales, and to the listener minor scales are in no way *heard* as "altered major scales." As a writer or an improvisor, musicians must learn to hear and use the different scale qualities to create melodies with the subtle emotional effects that give music its unique powers of expression.

NOTE: When comparing the A major and A minor scale structures, calling the lowered (or "natural") third, sixth, and seventh scale degrees "flat three," "flat six," and "flat seven" is technically incorrect. In everyday language, however, it is very common to use the terms "flat" and "sharp" to mean the same thing as "lowered" and "raised." This usage is acceptable so long as it is understood that, depending on the key signature, lowering a note does not always involve the use of a flat and raising a note does not always involve the use of a sharp, as these changes may also be accomplished with natural signs. (See Exercise 8.)

Pentatonic Scales

9

*P*entatonic scales are perhaps the most widely used scales in music. Found in the music of nearly all ancient cultures, today they are used in musical styles ranging from blues and rock to jazz and classical. The term "pentatonic" describes the number of tones in the scale—"penta" means five, and "tonic" refers to tones. Therefore, pentatonic scales contain five tones, as opposed to diatonic scales, which contain all seven tones of the musical alphabet. Although they contain fewer notes, the two pentatonic scales in common use still reflect the major and minor qualities of their diatonic counterparts.

Major Pentatonic Scales

Major pentatonic scales can be seen as major scales minus the fourth and seventh scale degrees, leaving the following notes: 1, 2, 3, 5, and 6.

Fig. 1: C major and C major pentatonic scales

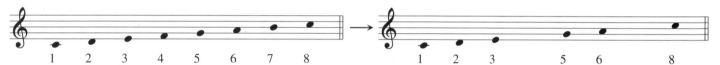

The major pentatonic scale has a simple, uncluttered sound and solves a problem that the diatonic major scale presents to untrained or inexperienced improvisors. The fourth and seventh scale degrees of the major scale, being a half step away from the third and octave respectively, have strong tendencies to resolve. If they are left unresolved without a clear purpose, as they often are when musicians first begin improvising, the resulting effect is unstable and incomplete. By eliminating these tones from the scale along with the half step intervals, the melodic difficulties are reduced, but the essence of the major quality remains. Melodies become much easier to manipulate, which accounts in part for the universal appeal of the pentatonic scale.

EXERCISE 1

Build major pentatonic scales on the staff in the following keys. Use accidentals where needed. In practice, the key signature of the diatonic major scale may be used when writing major pentatonic melodies.

Minor Pentatonic Scales

Minor pentatonic scales may be seen as the diatonic (natural) minor scale minus the second and sixth degrees, leaving the following notes: 1, ♭3, 4, 5, and ♭7.

Fig. 2: C natural minor and C minor pentatonic

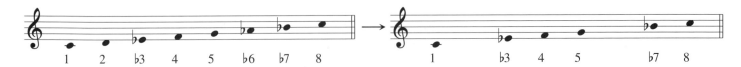

In natural minor scales, the fourth and seventh scale degrees are a whole step from the third and octave respectively, so they don't have the same tendency to resolve that these tones have in the major scale. However, the second scale degree (a half step below the minor third) and the sixth scale degree (a half step above the perfect fifth), if handled carelessly, can create the equivalent problem in minor keys. The minor pentatonic scale eliminates these half steps, yet still contains the essence of the minor quality and serves a function equivalent to the major pentatonic—that of a simple, straightforward scale for improvising and composing.

EXERCISE 2

Build minor pentatonic scales on the staff in the following keys. Use accidentals where needed. In practice, the key signature of the diatonic minor scale may be used when writing minor pentatonic melodies.

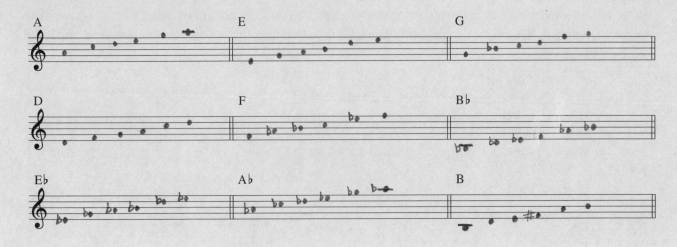

Part II:
Structures
Chords and Chord Progressions

The true study of harmony begins when chords are placed one after another to form progressions. While in the past, melodies were usually the essential ingredient around which a song would be built, today chord progressions and their related rhythms provide the basic structure of a great deal of popular music.

Popular music is still fairly conservative in its use of harmony. The diatonic system was mostly discarded years ago by classical and avant-garde jazz musicians, but it is still the main foundation of popular styles. The introduction of blues added elements that have bent the diatonic rules of harmony considerably, but the diatonic system remains the most important structure for understanding how chords are put together.

Other variations have developed in how the chords themselves are structured, with notes being added or altered within the basic qualities to form richer and often more dissonant sounds without going outside the diatonic system. Understanding this system is the key to understanding popular music, both as a player and as a writer.

Harmonizing
10 the Major Scale

Pentatonic scales are extremely popular and useful, but the diatonic major scale still provides the basis for how we construct and understand melodies in major keys. Likewise, the major scale is the basis for constructing and understanding major chord progressions. When harmonies are built by stacking the notes of the major scale in intervals of a third, the result is an organized system of chords called the *harmonized major scale*, also known as *diatonic harmony*. Many of the chord progressions heard in popular music are diatonic, and an understanding of diatonic harmony is the basis for understanding the harmony of all types of music.

Any major scale can be harmonized using the following method:

Step 1: Write out the scale, note for note.
We'll look at the C major scale as an example.

Step 2: Above each scale tone, write the scale tone that is a third interval higher in pitch.
That is, above C, write E; above D, write F, and so on through the scale. The scale is now "harmonized in thirds," resulting in a set of intervals in which all of the notes belong to the C major scale. Since the scale tones are not all the same distance apart, the third intervals vary in quality, with some major thirds and some minor thirds. Beneath the intervals, write the qualities of the thirds.

interval qualities: M   M   m   M   M   m   M

Step 3: Above each third interval, add the scale tone a fifth interval above the lowest note.
That is, above C and E, write G; above D and B, write A; and so on. This is the method for harmonizing the scale in triads. As you complete each triad, determine its quality and write it underneath the staff.

triads: M   m   m   M   M   m   d

EXERCISE 1

Harmonize the B♭ major scale in triads on the staff below, figure out the triad qualities, and write them underneath the staff. Remember the key signature!

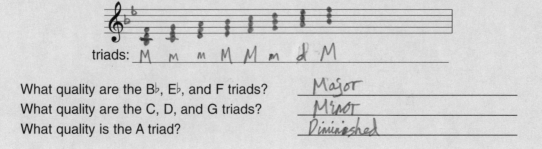

triads: M   m   m   M   M   m   d   M

What quality are the B♭, E♭, and F triads?	Major
What quality are the C, D, and G triads?	Minor
What quality is the A triad?	Diminished

Numbering Chords

It should be apparent that the order of chord qualities in each key is the same; only the names of the roots are different. Since all major scales are built in the same way, the same order of chord qualities will apply in every key. This allows us to derive a formula for chord qualities, eliminating the need to build harmonized scales one at a time.

As we have already used numbers to describe the position of single notes in a scale or chord, it is necessary to have a different type of numbering system when referring to complete chords. Scale degrees are identified by Arabic numbers (1, 2, 3...). Chords, however, are identified by *Roman numerals*, (I, II, III...). For example, the note E is the third degree (or simply "3rd") of the C major scale or a C major triad, while the E minor triad is called the "III chord" (pronounced "three chord") of the C major harmonized scale. Applying this system of chord numbering to the harmonized major scale yields the following formula:

Fig. 1: formula for the harmonized major scale

I   IImi   IIImi   IV   V   VImi   VII°

NOTE: One system of chord numbering uses upper- and lower-case Roman numerals to indicate chords and their qualities (e.g., I, ii, iii, IV, etc.). Another system uses all upper-case numerals followed by the chord quality, such as I, IImi, IIImi, IV, etc. There is no single system used by all musicians or music scholars. For the sake of clarity and consistency, we will use the latter system.

EXERCISE 2

Using the above formula, write the name of each triad in the harmonized scale of each key.

The Harmonized Major Scales

↓ Keys ↓	I	IImi	IIImi	IV	V	VImi	VII°
C major	C	Dmi	Emi	F	G	Ami	B°
F major	F	Gm	Am	B♭	C	Dm	E°
G major	G	Am	Bm	C	D	Em	F#°
B♭ major	B♭	Cm	Dm	E♭	F	Gm	A°
D major	D	Em	F#m	G	A	Bm	C#°
E♭ major	E♭	Fm	Gm	A♭	B♭	Cm	D°
A major	A	Bm	C#m	D	E	F#m	G#°
A♭ major	A♭	B♭m	Cm	D♭	E♭	Fm	G°
E major	E	F#m	G#m	A	B	C#m	D#°
D♭ major	D♭	E♭m	Fm	G♭	A♭	B♭m	C°
B major	B	C#m	D#m	E	F#	G#m	A#°

EXERCISE 3

1. *Without consulting the previous harmonized scale table*, name these triads:

IV chord of E♭ major	A♭	IIImi chord of G major	Bm
V chord of A major	E	VImi chord of B♭ major	Gm
IImi chord of D major	Em	IImi chord of F major	Gm
VII° chord of A♭ major	G°	V chord of E major	B
IIImi chord of B major	D#m	VII° chord of D♭ major	C°
VImi chord of A major	F#m	IV chord of C major	F

2. Each of the chords below is a IV chord; name the key to which it belongs.

B♭: F Major A: E Major E♭: B Major

D♭: A♭ Major G: D Major D: A Major

3. Each of these chords is a VImi chord; name the key to which it belongs.

Bmi: D Major C#mi: E Major B♭mi: D♭ Major

E♭mi: G♭ Major G#mi: B Major Fmi: A♭ Major

EXERCISE 4

Write the following chord progressions in the keys indicated.

1. Progression: I IV V I

Key:					
	C:	C	F	G	C
	F:	F	B♭	C	F
	G:	G	C	D	G

2. Progression: I VImi IImi V

Key:					
	B♭:	B♭	Gm	Cm	F
	D:	D	Bm	Em	A
	E♭:	E♭	Cm	Fm	B♭

3. Progression: I IIImi VImi IV

Key:					
	A:	A	C#m	F#m	D
	A♭:	A♭	Cm	Fm	D♭
	E:	E	G#m	C#m	A

EXERCISE 5

Convert the chords to Roman numerals in the keys indicated.

1. Key of F: F Bb C F

numerals: I IV V I

2. Key of G: G Emi C D

numerals: I vi IV V

3. Key of Bb: Bb Gmi Cmi F

numerals: I vi ii V

4. Key of D: D F#mi Bmi G

numerals: I iii vi IV

5. Key of A: C#mi F#mi Bmi E

numerals: iii vi ii V

Transposition

When a formula exists that is the same for all keys, it becomes possible to play a melody or progression in any key by converting the notes or chords in one key to numbers, then converting those numbers back to notes or chords in the new key. The relationships will all be identical; only the note names will change. Moving a melody or progression from key to key is called *transposing*, and the ability to transpose is important for composers, accompanists, and improvisors alike. The use of number relationships combined with the knowledge of how to play an instrument in all keys allows a piece of music to be quickly and accurately transposed on the spot.

EXERCISE 6

Translate each of the following progressions into Roman numerals, then transpose them to the key of C major.

1.   F C Dmi Bb E° Ami Gmi C

numerals: I V vi IV vii° iii ii V

key of C: C G Am F B° Em Dm G

EXERCISE 6 (cont'd)

2.

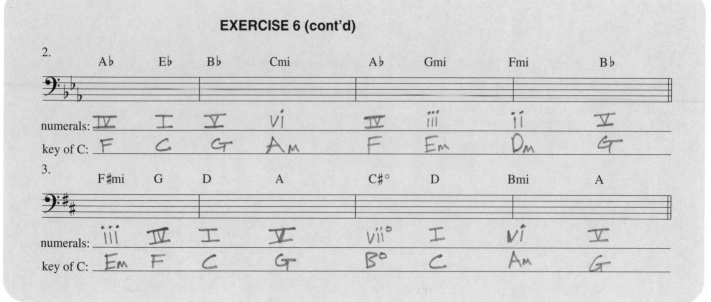

	Ab	Eb	Bb	Cmi	Ab	Gmi	Fmi	Bb
numerals:	IV	I	V	vi	IV	iii	ii	V
key of C:	F	C	G	Am	F	Em	Dm	G

3.

	F#mi	G	D	A	C#°	D	Bmi	A
numerals:	iii	IV	I	V	vii°	I	vi	V
key of C:	Em	F	C	G	B°	C	Am	G

EXERCISE 7

Translate each of the following melodies into numbers by finding the scale step number of each note in relation to its key signature. One melody is in a major key, and the other is in a minor key—look at the melodies closely in relation to the key signature to figure out which is which. After you have figured out the numbers, transpose the major melody into the key of C major and the minor melody into A minor.

1.

scale steps: 1 5 6 3 5 3 4 3 2 3 1

2.

scale steps: 1 5 6 5 4 3 4 2 3 4 3 2 3 1

Harmonizing the Minor Scale

11

As we have seen in previous chapters, the natural minor scale serves as the source of diatonic melodies in minor keys just as the major scale is the source of diatonic melodies in major keys. Likewise, the *harmonized natural minor scale* is the source of diatonic harmony in minor keys. Minor and major scales are harmonized using exactly the same method, illustrated here:

Step 1: Write out the scale, note for note.

We'll look at the A natural minor scale as an example.

Step 2: Above each scale tone, write the scale tone that is a third interval higher in pitch.

That is, above A, write C; above B, write D; and so on through the scale. The scale is now "harmonized in thirds," resulting in a set of intervals in which all of the notes belong to the A minor scale. Since the scale tones are not all the same distance apart, the third intervals vary in quality, with some minor thirds and some major thirds. Beneath the intervals, write the qualities of the thirds.

interval qualities:

Step 3: Above each third interval, add the scale tone a fifth above the lowest note.

That is, above A and C, write E; above B and D, write F; and so on. The scale is now harmonized in triads. As you complete each triad, identify its quality and write it underneath the staff.

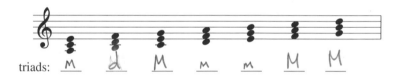

triads:

EXERCISE 1

Harmonize the G minor scale in triads on the staff below, figure out the triad qualities, and write them underneath the staff. Remember the key signature!

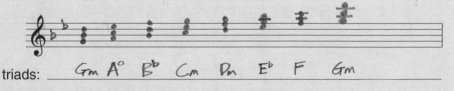

triads: _Gm A° B♭ Cm Dm E♭ F Gm_

What quality are the G, C, D, and triads? _Minor_

What quality are the B♭, E♭, and F triads? _Major_

What quality is the A triad? _Diminished_

Based on harmonizing these two scales, it is clear that the same idea that applied to harmonizing the major scale also applies to harmonizing the minor scale: the chord qualities occur in exactly the same order regardless of key. As a result, we can derive a formula for chord qualities that will be the same for all harmonized natural minor scales.

Fig. 1: formula for the harmonized minor scale

$$\text{Imi} \quad \text{II}° \quad ♭\text{III} \quad \text{IVmi} \quad \text{Vmi} \quad ♭\text{VI} \quad ♭\text{VII}$$

NOTE: When numbering scale tones in minor keys, it is common to compare them to major scale tones, in other words, the third degree of the A minor scale, C, is typically called "♭3" ("flat three"), while the third degree of the A major scale, C♯, is called simply "3." The same practice applies to numbering chords. The third chord in the harmonized A minor scale, C major, is labeled "♭III" ("flat three major"), while the third chord in the harmonized major scale, C♯ minor, is labeled "iiimi" ("three minor"). Keep in mind that the terms "flat" and "sharp" are used here in the general sense of "lowered" and "raised"—whether or not an actual flat or sharp sign is appropriate will depend on the key signature.

Just as each minor scale has a relative major scale that shares the same key signature, minor and major scale harmonies are also relative. The same triads that are found in the key of A minor are also found in the key of C major. This does not mean that the two keys are "the same" except that they share the same key signature; each is a complete system built around its own tonic. Since they do share the key signature, however, some time can be saved at first in locating the specific names of notes and chords in minor keys by comparing them to the relative major. Once you have gained some experience with minor keys, it will become easier to see them on their own, apart from major.

EXERCISE 2

Using the formula, write the name of each triad in the harmonized minor scale.

The Harmonized Minor Scales

↓ Keys ↓	Imi	II°	♭III	IVmi	Vmi	♭VI	♭VII
A minor	Ami	B°	C	Dmi	Emi	F	G
D minor	Dm	E°	F	Gm	Am	B♭	C
E minor	Em	F#°	G	Am	Bm	C	D
G minor	Gm	A°	B♭	Cm	Dm	E♭	F
B minor	Bm	C#°	D	Em	F#m	G	A
C minor	Cm	D°	E♭	Fm	Gm	A♭	B♭
F# minor	F#m	G#°	A	Bm	C#m	D	E
F minor	Fm	G°	♭A	B♭m	Cm	D♭	E♭
C# minor	C#m	D#°	E	F#m	G#m	A	B
B♭ minor	B♭m	C°	♭D	E♭m	Fm	G♭	A♭
G# minor	G#m	A#°	B	C#m	D#m	E	F#

Chapter 11

EXERCISE 3

1. *Without consulting the previous harmonized scale table*, name these triads:

IVmi chord of C minor	Fm	♭III chord of E minor	G
Vmi chord of F♯ minor	C♯m	♭VI chord of B♭ minor	G♭
II° chord of B minor	C♯°	II° chord of D minor	E°
♭VII chord of F minor	E♭	Vmi chord of C♯ minor	G♯m
♭III chord of G♯ minor	B	♭VII chord of B♭ minor	A♭
♭VI chord of F♯ minor	D	IVmi chord of A minor	Dm

2. Each of the chords below is a ♭III chord. Name the minor key to which it belongs:

B♭: G Minor   G: E Minor   A: C♯ Minor
D♭: B♭ Minor   C: A Minor   D: B Minor

3. Each of the chords below is a Vmi chord. Name the minor key to which it belongs:

Bmi: E Minor   C♯mi: F♯ Minor   B♭mi: E♭ Minor
E♭mi: A♭ Minor G♯mi: D♯ Minor   Fmi: B♭ Minor

EXERCISE 4

Write the following chord progressions in the keys indicated.

1. **Progression:**

		Imi	IVmi	Vmi	Imi
Key:	G minor:	Gm	Cm	Dm	Gm
	C minor:	Cm	Fm	Gm	Cm
	D minor:	Dm	Gm	Am	Dm

2. **Progression:**

		Imi	♭VI	♭VII	Vmi
Key:	F minor:	Fm	D♭	E♭	Cm
	A minor:	Am	F	G	Em
	B♭ minor:	B♭m	G♭	A♭	Fm

3. **Progression:**

		Imi	♭III	II°	Vmi
Key:	F♯ minor:	F♯m	A	G♯°	C♯m
	C♯ minor:	C♯m	E	D♯°	G♯m
	B minor:	Bm	D	C♯°	F♯m

EXERCISE 5

Convert the chords to Roman numerals in the keys indicated.

1. Key of G minor: Gmi   E♭   B♭   Dmi

   numerals: Iₘ   V ♭VI   ♭III   Vₘ

2. Key of B minor: Bmi   Emi   C♯°   F♯mi

   numerals: Iₘ   IVₘ   II°   Vₘ

3. Key of C♯ minor: C♯mi   E   A   F♯mi

   numerals: Iₘ   ♭III   ♭VI   IVₘ

4. Key of F minor: Fmi   Cmi   D♭   E♭

   numerals: Iₘ   Vₘ   ♭VI   ♭VII

5. Key of E minor: Emi   D   G   Bmi

   numerals: Iₘ   ♭VII   ♭III   Vₘ

EXERCISE 6

Translate each of the following progressions into numbers, then transpose them to the key of A minor.

1.
Dmi	Ami	F	Gmi	C	F	E°	Ami

numbers: Iₘ   Vₘ   ♭III   IVₘ   ♭VII   ♭III   II°   Vₘ

key of A minor: Aₘ Eₘ   C   Dₘ   G   C   B°   Eₘ

2.
Fmi	Cmi	Gmi	A♭	Fmi	E♭	D°	Gmi

numbers: IVₘ   Iₘ   Vₘ   ♭VI   IVₘ   ♭III   II°   Vₘ

key of A minor: Dₘ Aₘ   Eₘ   F   Dₘ   C   B   Eₘ

3.
D	Emi	Bmi	F♯mi	A	Bmi	G	F♯mi

numbers: ♭III   IVₘ   Iₘ   Vₘ   VII   Iₘ   VI   Vₘ

key of A minor: C Dₘ   Aₘ   Eₘ   G   Aₘ   F   Eₘ

Diatonic Seventh Chords

12

iatonic triads have a direct emotional quality that makes them very well suited for much of popular harmony, especially rock. When a fourth diatonic note, the seventh, is added to each of the diatonic triads, a more complex sound is created that is both more dissonant and more emotionally subtle. The resulting chords, called *diatonic seventh chords*, define the fundamental harmony of styles such as blues and jazz.

Building Diatonic Seventh Chords

The first step in learning to build diatonic seventh chords is to expand the harmonization of the major and minor scales by adding a seventh interval to each of the diatonic triads.

EXERCISE 1

Harmonize the C major scale, adding a seventh to each of the triads.

When the results of harmonizing the C major scale in sevenths are analyzed, there are four different seventh chord qualities that result:

1. **The I and IV chords** are both *major* triads with the addition of a *major* seventh degree above the root (the intervals C–B and F–E). They are called *major seventh chords.*

2. **The ii, iii, and vi chords** are all *minor* triads with the addition of a *minor seventh* degree above the root (the intervals D–C, E–D, and A–G). They are called *minor seventh chords.*

3. The V chord is a *major* triad with the addition of a *minor* seventh degree above the root (the interval G–F). It is called a *dominant seventh chord.*

4. The VII chord is a *diminished* triad with the addition of a *minor* seventh degree above the root (the interval B–A). It is called a *minor seven flat five chord.*

Compare the construction of the diatonic seventh chord and triad qualities when based on the same root. This will show how the differences in interval quality within each chord affect the overall chord structure.

EXERCISE 2

Write each chord type on the staff based on the root C.

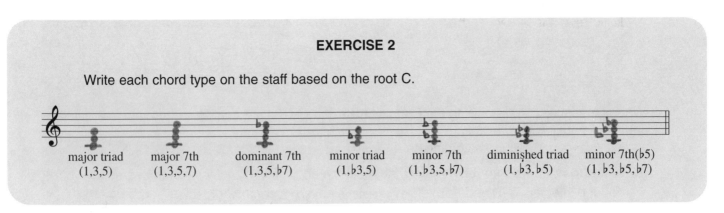

EXERCISE 3

Build these seventh chords on the staff.

Chapter 12

Harmonizing the Major Scale in Sevenths

When the C major scale is harmonized in sevenths, the result is a certain order of chord qualities. Since all major scales are built according to the same formula, this order will be the same in all keys, just as it was for diatonic triads.

Fig. 1: formula for the harmonized major scale in sevenths

Ima7   IImi7   IIImi7   IVma7   V7   VImi7   VIImi7(♭5)

Notice that the names "major seventh" and "minor seventh" are nearly the same as the names of triad qualities built on the same scale degrees. The other two seventh chord names, the V7 ("dominant seventh") and the VIImi7(♭5) ("minor seven flat five"), are different from those of the triads built on the same degrees. Simply remembering which chord names are similar to those of the diatonic triads and which are different makes it unnecessary to create a table of all of the seventh chords in every key.

Harmonizing the Natural Minor Scale in Sevenths

Adding sevenths to each of the diatonic triads in the harmonized natural minor scale is done by the same procedure that was applied to the major scale.

EXERCISE 4

Harmonize the C minor scale, adding a seventh to each of the triads. Underneath the staff, label each seventh chord, including its quality.

quality: Cm7   Dm7(♭5)   E♭M7   Fm7   Gm7   A♭M7   B♭7

There are four seventh chord qualities, just as in the harmonized major scale, but in a different order. Since all natural minor scales are identically constructed, the same order of qualities will result for any key, allowing the creation of a formula.

Fig. 2: formula for the harmonized minor scale in sevenths

Imi7   IImi7(♭5)   ♭IIImaj7   IVmi7   Vmi7   ♭VIma7   ♭VII7

Again, as in the comparison of the diatonic triads and seventh chords in major keys, remembering which names are similar and which are different eliminates the need to list all seventh chords in all keys separately. To name any seventh chord in any key, major or minor:

1. Use the key signature to identify the root.
2. Add the chord quality that belongs with that scale step.

EXERCISE 5

Based on the scale harmony formulas for major and minor keys, find the names of the indicated *seventh* chords.

1. Name the V chord in the key of:

| F major | C7 | E major | B7 | E minor | Bm7 |
| A major | C7 | D minor | Am7 | G minor | Dm7 |

2. Name the VI chord in the key of:

| G major | Em7 | Bb major | Gm7 | F minor | DM7 |
| D major | Bm7 | A minor | FM7 | B minor | G#M7 |

3. Name the II chord in the key of:

| Eb major | Fm7 | B major | C#m7 | F# minor | G#m7(b5) |
| Ab major | Bbm7 | C minor | Dm7(b5) | G# minor | A#m7(b5) |

4. Name the IV chord in the key of:

| A major | DM7 | Eb major | AbM7 | F minor | Bbm7 |
| G major | CM7 | G minor | Cm7 | C minor | Fm7 |

5. Name the III chord in the key of:

| F major | Am7 | Bb major | Dm7 | E minor | GM7 |
| D major | F#m7 | D minor | FM7 | B minor | D#M7 |

6. Name the VII chord in the key of:

| Ab major | Gm7(b5) | C major | Bm7(b5) | A minor | G7 |
| B major | A#m7(b5) | F# minor | E7 | G# minor | F#7 |

Key Centers

13

Musicians in the field of popular music are routinely required to work with chord charts that are not accompanied by key signatures, or that change key at some point during a piece of music without a change in the written key signature. In order to create a melody, improvise, or play a melodic bass line in such a situation, it is necessary to be able to tell what key a progression belongs to by means of the chords alone. Listening to the piece and finding the key by ear is generally the most musical approach, but it is also possible to see what key the progression is in by analyzing the chords to find out how many belong to the same harmonized scale. Locating the single key that a group of chords have in common is called finding the *key center*.

Finding Major Key Centers

The method for finding the key center of a chord progression is as follows:

Step 1: Look at each of the chords in the progression, and list the keys to which they could belong based on their quality. Since the harmonized major scale contains three minor seventh chords (IImi7, IIImi7, and VImi7), each minor seventh chord could belong to any of three different keys. The major seventh chords could be either Ima7 or IVma7 of two different keys, and the dominant seventh chord will be V7 of one key only.

	Emi7	Cma7	Ami7	D7	Gma7
possible keys:	D	C	G	G	G
	C	G	F		D
	G		C		

Step 2: Compare the possible keys to find the one key to which all of the chords belong. This is the key center of the progression. What is it? *G Major*

Step 3: Below the staff, write the Roman numeral for each chord as it relates to the key center. The Roman numeral of a chord is commonly referred to as its chord *function.*

	Emi7	Cma7	Ami7	D7	Gma7
function:	VImi7	IVma7	IImi7	V7	Ima7

From the example above, it is clear that the quickest indicator of the key center is the dominant seventh chord, as it is found in only one place in the harmonized major scale. In fact, the V7–I progression is the most common in music, with the dissonant V7 chord creating a feeling of motion toward the consonant I chord. Because it is so common, it is nearly guaranteed to appear in any progression that includes seventh chords. As a rule, when analyzing a progression, first identify the key to which the dominant seventh chord belongs, then check the other chords to confirm that they also belong to the same key.

EXERCISE 1

Find the key center of the following progression, and identify the function of each chord, writing it below the staff.

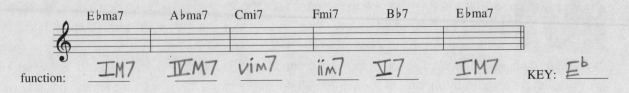

Ebma7	Abma7	Cmi7	Fmi7	Bb7	Ebma7

function: IM7   IVM7   vim7   iim7   V7   IM7   KEY: Eb

EXERCISE 2

This progression contains several different key centers. Identify the function of each chord, and write it below the staff, bracketing the key centers above the staff as shown.

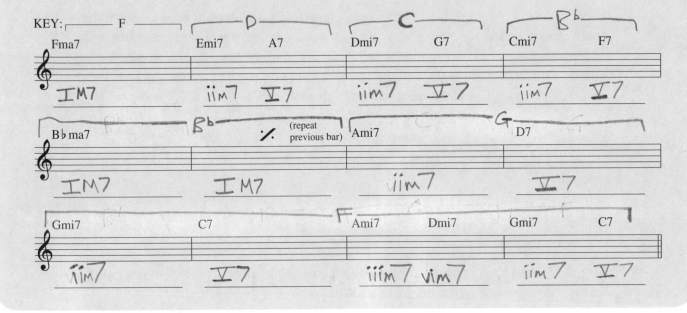

KEY: ⌐——— F ———⌐ ⌐——— D ———⌐ ⌐—— C ——⌐ ⌐—— Bb ——⌐

Fma7   Emi7   A7   Dmi7   G7   Cmi7   F7

IM7   iim7   V7   iim7   V7   iim7   V7

Bbma7   (repeat previous bar)   Ami7   D7

IM7   IM7   iim7   V7

Gmi7   C7   Ami7   Dmi7   Gmi7   C7

iim7   V7   iiim7   vim7   iim7   V7

Identifying Minor Key Centers

In theory, minor key centers can be identified using exactly the same technique; in the natural minor harmonized scale, the dominant seventh chord is a ♭VII7 chord rather than a V7 chord, but it still belongs to only a single key and therefore points directly to the key center.

Fig. 1: natural minor chord progression

Cmi7	Abma7	Fmi7	Bb7	Cmi7

function: Imi7   ♭VIma7   IVmi7   ♭VII7   Imi7   KEY: C minor

In practice, things are somewhat more complicated in minor keys. For reasons that will be explained more fully at a later point, the natural minor scale and its harmonies are often altered in order to create more powerful and pleasing melodies and chord progressions. One result of this alteration is that very often the V chord in minor keys is changed from a minor seventh chord to a dominant seventh chord, making the specific function of the dominant chord less clear to the eye. It becomes necessary to look for interval relationships between chords, that is:

- If there is a minor chord a whole step above the dominant seventh chord, then the dominant seventh chord is ♭VII7 and the minor seventh chord is Imi7, as seen in Figure 1.

- If there is a minor seventh chord a perfect fifth below the dominant seventh chord, then the dominant seventh chord is V7 and the minor seventh chord is Imi7, as seen here:

	Gmi7	E♭ma7	Cmi7	D7	Gmi7	
function:	Imi7	♭VIma7	IVmi7	V7	Imi7	KEY: G minor

Another quick indicator of the key center in minor keys is the *minor seven flat five chord*. This chord, if it is used in the progression, functions exclusively as a II° chord in the natural minor scale harmony. This makes the minor seven flat five chord the most obvious visual indicator of the key center in minor keys. (In practice, the minor seven flat five chord is only rarely seen as a VII° chord in major keys.)

EXERCISE 3

Analyze the function of each chord, and locate the key center.

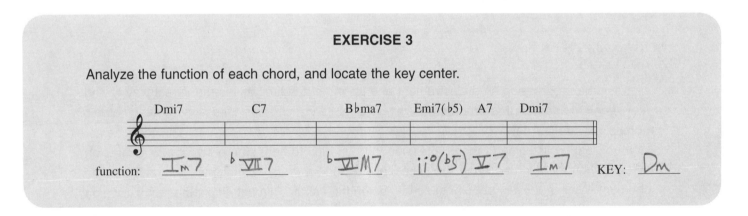

	Dmi7	C7	B♭ma7	Emi7(♭5)	A7	Dmi7	
function:	Im7	♭VII7	♭VIM7	ii°(♭5)	V7	Im7	KEY: Dm

Finding Key Centers in Triad Progressions

We have identified the dominant seventh chord and the minor seven flat five chord as the easiest ways to locate key centers in major or minor keys. In popular styles like rock, however, it is very common for progressions to be made up exclusively of triads, which means that the V chord is a major triad, just like the IV and I chords. Also, in triad progressions it is unusual for the diminished triad (VII° in major keys, II° in minor keys) to appear at all, since it is much more dissonant than the major and minor triads that make up the rest of the scale harmony and therefore sounds out of place.

The question is, then, how may the key center be identified when each chord could theoretically have more than one function? The answer can be found in two ways.

A. Rearrange the chords into a scalewise order

In the exercise below, each of the chords could theoretically belong to at least two different keys. When arranged into a harmonized scale, though, they only fit together into one pattern. Finding the correct key involves a process of trial and error. Begin by guessing which chord is likely to be I and seeing if the rest of the chords fit into its scale harmony. If not, try another potential I chord until you find the one with which the rest of the chords make sense.

EXERCISE 4

Rearrange the chords in the progression below until you find the single scale harmony to which they all belong. Only one key contains all of the chords, so experiment until you find the actual I chord. When you find it, write the chord names and functions in the spaces provided.

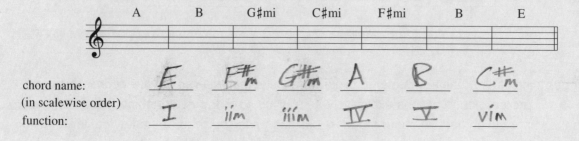

chord name:
(in scalewise order)

E	F#m	G#m	A	B	C#m

function:

I	iim	iiim	IV	V	vim

B. Use your ear

Play the progression on an instrument and listen. In practice, this is the surest way to find a key center whether the progression includes seventh chords, triads, or both. Diatonic progressions are by definition tonal, revolving around a single tone center. The tone center becomes clear by listening to the progression long enough to hear where it *resolves* (settles on the tonic chord), then identifying the name of the tone center by matching that note on an instrument. While not every popular song begins on the I chord, almost all popular songs *end* on the I chord. Play each of the progressions in this chapter on a keyboard or guitar to find out how quickly you can hear the key center. Sing the note, match it on your instrument, and check to see that it is the same as what you found by analyzing the chords.

Finding key centers by sight alone is difficult in many cases, and some experience is required before it becomes an efficient method. The process of training the ear is partly a process of learning to *hear* what you *see,* so that when you actually begin to play, you already know the outcome. The combination of education and a trained ear allows a musician to be both knowledgable and musical, two essential ingredients of a versatile career.

Blues

14

The process of identifying key centers in diatonic major and minor chord progressions is generally fairly simple once you have some experience. In most cases, a dominant seventh chord points the way directly to the tonic chord, and the other chords may then be quickly analyzed.

However, modern harmony is often not entirely diatonic, and there are a certain number of variations that must be understood for you to have much success at analyzing progressions in the "real world." The remainder of your studies in the field of harmony and theory will deal predominantly with exceptions to the straightforward rules of diatonic harmony and melody. The first such exception is *blues.*

Blues Harmony

Blues is a style that combines elements of African and European musical traditions in a unique blend that defies analysis by classically-based methods.

The three basic chords in blues are the same as the three basic chords in the diatonic system: I, IV, and V. What sets blues harmony apart from traditional Western European harmony is the quality of the sevenths. We have been taught to recognize dominant seventh chords as V chords related to a single tonic, but in blues, all three chords are dominant sevenths; that is, the I and IV chords as well as the V chord are dominant-quality chords. In blues, the fact that all of these chords are dominant sevenths does not imply the existence of three different keys; briefly listening to a blues progression will make it obvious that, despite the chord qualities, there is clearly a single tonic chord, and the other chords function in essentially the same way that they do in diatonic progressions. While the use of the dominant seventh chord outside its diatonic role was first heard by classically-trained musicians as dissonant and unresolved, it is now accepted as normal.

The chords in blues are generally arranged in one of several traditional progressions that evolved around the beginning of the twentieth century, according to available information. The first and by far the most common of these progressions is the *twelve-bar blues*. This progression remains essentially the same regardless of key or tempo, and is most usefully learned by memorizing the order of chords and the number of bars for each. It can then be transposed into any key on any instrument.

Fig. 1: the twelve-bar blues

repeat entire progression

| I7 | ./. | ./. | ./. | IV7 | ./. | I7 | ./. | V7 | IV7 | I7 | V7 |

EXERCISE 1

Transpose the twelve-bar blues progression into each of the following keys, writing the proper chord names above the appropriate bars.

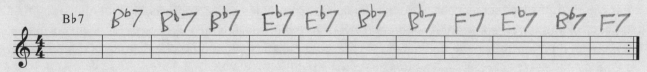

Bb7   B♭7   B♭7   B♭7   E♭7   E♭7   B♭7   B♭7   F7   E♭7   B♭7   F7

EXERCISE 1 (cont'd)

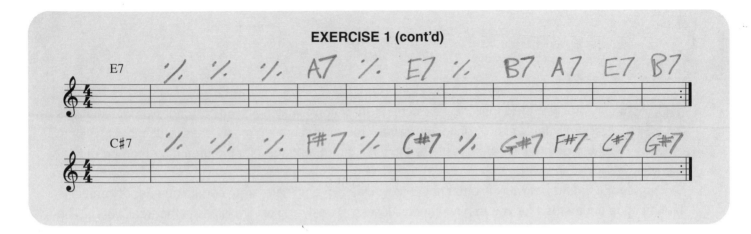

Another traditional progression is the *eight-bar blues*. It actually comes in several different varieties, but the two most common variations are as follows.

Fig. 2: eight-bar blues progressions

A.

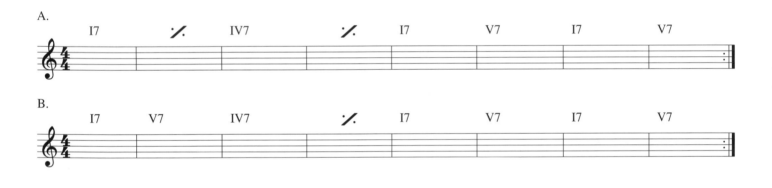

B.

EXERCISE 2

Transpose the first eight-bar blues progression above into the key of G major.

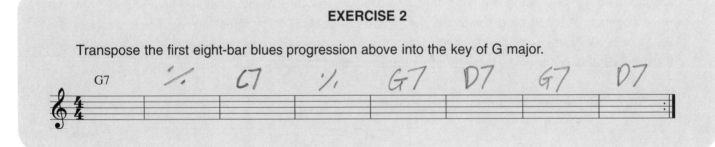

In both the twelve-bar and eight-bar progressions, only I7, IV7, and V7 chords are used. Notice that in each case, the progression begins on the I7 chord and appears to end on the V7 chord. In reality, these progressions are intended to be played over and over, so the last V7 (called the *turnaround*) actually does resolve to the first I7 chord when the progression repeats. Although all three chords share the same quality, the tonality is obvious due to the strong root movement between I7, IV7, and V7 that points the ear clearly to the correct function. This is true also in other blues-style progressions that may add other chords, use other chord arrangements, and even vary the qualities of the chords (as in *minor blues*, where the I, IV, and V chords are all minor). The relationship of I, IV, and V is so strong that it binds the harmony together despite these variations.

Chapter 14

Blues Melody

One of the unique, striking aspects of blues is the sound of the melody. Again, it breaks the rules we have established regarding the diatonic relationship between the melody and harmony. Just as the blues progression is technically nondiatonic yet sounds nearly as direct and tonal as the harmonized major scale, blues melody is unlike either the diatonic major or minor scale yet also sounds just as tonal. Actual blues melodies defy traditional musical notation by including sounds that literally fall between the notes on the staff, but they can be simplified somewhat and organized into a set of notes called the *blues scale*. The blues scale most closely resembles the minor pentatonic scale with the addition of an extra note commonly called the *flatted fifth*. (Also called the "flat five," this note is technically a diminished fifth or augmented fourth, depending on context, but in blues is rarely referred to by those names.)

Fig. 3: the blues scale

scale steps: 1   ♭3   4   ♭5   5   ♭7   8

EXERCISE 3

Write blues scales on the staff in each of the following keys.

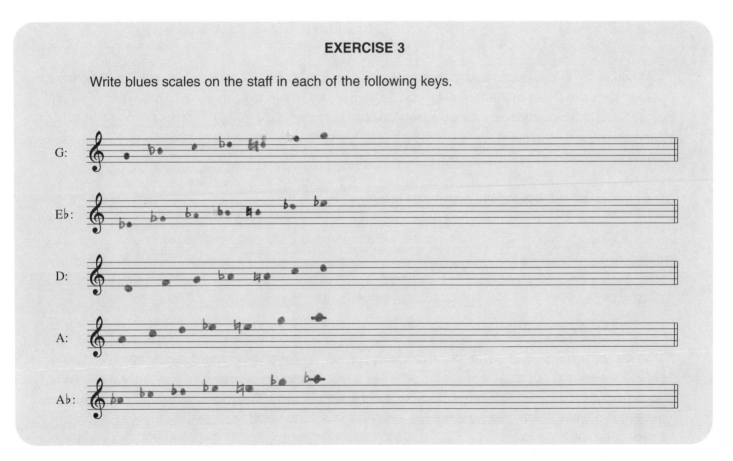

The uniqueness of the blues scale lies in the *blue notes*, those notes in the scale that technically clash with the harmony. Since the blues scale is used primarily over dominant seventh chords, one would expect the scale to match the sound of the chord. However, the blues scale contains two notes that actually clash with notes of the dominant seventh chord, creating a melodic dissonance that is a trademark of blues. These two "blue" notes are the *minor third* and the *flat five*. Placing emphasis on these "wrong" notes is much of what makes blues sound "bluesy." (The *minor seventh* is also sometimes considered a blue note, although it is already part of the dominant chord.)

In practice, many players and singers add other notes to the blues scale to create more elaborate, diatonic-sounding melodies, but the essence of blues melody still lies in the blues scale itself.

Blues Rhythm

Blues rhythm is also distinctive, although not unique to blues in the same way that the blues progression and the blues scale are. It is traditionally based on a rhythm called the *eighth-note triplet shuffle.*

The eighth-note triplet shuffle, or simply "shuffle," is created by combining the first two notes of an eighth-note triplet into a single, longer note and leaving the third note short, resulting in a lopsided but relaxed rhythmic figure that is closely identified with blues.

Fig. 4: the eighth-note triplet shuffle

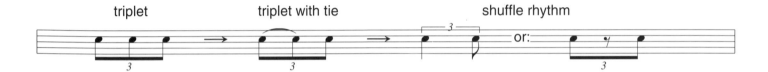

When seen on chord charts, the shuffle rhythm is usually notated either by simply writing the word "shuffle" above the staff at the top, near the clef sign, or by using notation showing that normal eighth notes should be interpreted with a shuffle feel. This saves the trouble and visual confusion of writing triplet rhythms throughout the piece.

Fig. 5: chart symbol indicating shuffle interpretation

It should be noted that the shuffle feel, when applied in jazz, is interpreted stylistically in a manner commonly called *swing.* The term "swing" also has a more general meaning of a relaxed, yet emphatic, sense of rhythm. In terms of harmony, melody, and rhythm, blues and jazz have remained closely related during their common evolution over the last century.

Chord Inversion

U p to this point, our study of harmony has concentrated on learning how to build various chords by stacking intervals above the root as well as on understanding diatonic relationships (knowing which chord qualities have their roots on which scale degrees). These are basic facts of popular harmony, yet in the real world these structures and relationships are continually being manipulated in various ways to create more variety without losing the underlying sense of tonality. The chapter on blues showed one way in which diatonic rules are stretched to inject different types of feeling into harmony. In this chapter, we will look more closely at how chords may be literally turned upside-down to create still more richness and variety without changing their basic diatonic quality.

Chord Voicings

So far, all of the chords we have studied have been constructed the same way: with the root as the lowest note and each higher note stacked in order, producing either three-note chords (triads) or four-note chords (seventh chords). This is the clearest way to see the chord qualities and understand how those qualities fit together to form diatonic progressions. In practice, however, chords are not always built the same way. Depending on the nature of a given instrument, the skill of the player, or the intention of the composer, the notes of a chord may be rearranged in several different ways. The actual arrangement of the notes of a chord in vertical order above the lowest note is called the *voicing.* The notes of a chord may be thought of as being similar to individual voices, with each one movable to a different position in relation to the others. In most cases, the root remains in the bass while the upper voices are rearranged. A chord with the root in the bass, regardless of the order of the upper voices, is described as being in *root position.*

EXERCISE 1

Write the root position triads on the staff beneath the given chord voicings. The voicings are written from the lowest to the highest note (e.g., "1, 5, 3" means that the root is in the bass, the next note above the root is the fifth, and the highest note is the third). The qualities of the third and fifth must match the quality of the chord. In some cases, a certain voice may be used more than once; if so, construct the chord so that the repeated voices are in different octaves.

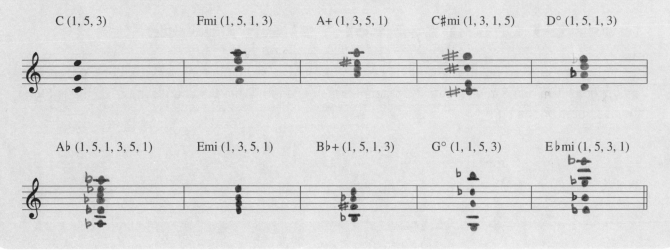

Chord Inversion

A basic principle of chord voicing states that the notes of a chord may be arranged in any order without affecting the quality of the chord. This may involve rearranging the upper notes while staying in root position, or it may also mean placing a note other than the root in the bass. The second option is called *chord inversion*, that is, "inverting" the chord, or turning it on its head. There are three possible inversions, in addition to root position:

first inversion: a chord voicing with the third chord degree in the bass
second inversion: a chord voicing with the fifth chord degree in the bass
third inversion: a chord voicing with the seventh chord degree in the bass

Triads may only be voiced in first or second inversion, while a seventh chord may be voiced in all three inversions. The inversion refers only to which note is in the bass; the upper notes may still be voiced in any order.

EXERCISE 2

Voice the triads in the indicated inversions above the given pitches. Include all necessary notes and maintain the proper chord qualities. For first inversion chords, the given pitch is the third chord degree; add the fifth and root above it. For second inversion chords, the given pitch is the fifth chord degree; add the root and third above it.

Inverted Chord Symbols: Slash Chords

In popular musical notation, inverted chords are represented by the following symbol, known as a *slash chord*. The name comes from the diagonal slash used to divide the chord symbol on the left from the bass note on the right.

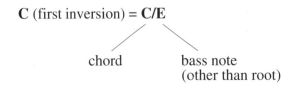

Chapter 15

EXERCISE 3

Modify the chord symbols from Exercise 2 using slash chord notation. For example, the first inversion D chord would be notated by adding a slash and the letter name of the bass note:

First inversion:

D/F#   B♭/D   E°/G   Gm/B♭   F#/A#   A°/C   A+/C   Bm/D

Second inversion:

A+/E#   C°/G♭   B♭m/F   E♭/B♭   B/F#   D°/A♭   C#m/G#   E+/B#

EXERCISE 4

Write the inverted seventh chords (notated with slash chord symbols) on the staff. Compare the bass note to the chord to identify which inversion you are building.

Fma7/E	B♭7/D	Ami7/E	E♭7/B♭
inversion: 3rd	1st	2nd	2nd

B7/A	F#mi7/C#	Dmi7(♭5)/C	A♭mi7/E♭
3rd	2nd	3rd	2nd

Cmi7/B♭	Emi7/G	Gma7/B	C#mi7(♭5)/G
3rd	1st	1st	2nd

Identifying Chord Inversions on the Staff

When an inverted chord is written on the staff in musical notation, the true name of the chord may be identified by rearranging the notes of the chord until they are stacked in third intervals (as close together as possible). Once this is done, the lowest note will automatically be the root. Then the inversion can be identified and a slash chord symbol used if necessary.

EXERCISE 5

Rewrite the following chords in root position, and name them using slash chord notation.

Voice Leading

The reason for rearranging the individual voices of a chord into inversions is to create more possibilities for chord connection. The study of smooth chord connection and the principles by which it is achieved is called *voice leading*. The term refers to the idea that the individual notes (or voices) of a chord progression should connect (or lead) smoothly by way of the nearest tone, from one chord to the next. The most obvious effect of inverting a chord is to change its bass note, and one result of voice leading through the use of inversions is the creation of melodic bass lines that connect from chord to chord by steps rather than by the wider leaps common when root position voicings alone are used.

EXERCISE 6

Write the following progression on the staff in two different ways. First, write the chords in root position only. Then, use the combination of root position chords and inversions indicated by the slash chord symbols.

In the second example, the notes are visually more connected due to the fact that the bass line forms a stepwise melody. A thorough study of bass lines and voice leading is a big part of learning to compose and arrange. Knowing how to build inverted chords and to recognize them on the staff is a very important first step.

16 Extended Chords

Any discussion of harmony must take into account the two ways we perceive it, that is, as both the structure of individual chords (commonly known as *vertical harmony*) and as the relationship of chords to each other within a progression (or *horizontal harmony*). During the rest of this book, we will continue to explore both views of harmony, going beyond triads, seventh chord structures, and diatonic chord progressions to include the more complex, or at least more difficult to explain, chords and progressions found in popular harmony.

Compound Intervals

To be able to describe other types of chords, we need to first look again at intervals. Our original discussion of intervals dealt only with interval quantities up to an octave, and, so far, all of the scales and chords covered in this book have been built within that limit. However, intervals beyond the octave are commonly used in popular harmony, so we need to expand our terminology to include these larger quantities.

In traditional terminology, intervals within the octave are called *simple intervals*. When intervals extend beyond an octave, they are called *compound intervals* because they are built from an octave plus a simple interval, as shown in this chart:

Fig. 1: compound intervals

octave	+	simple interval	=	compound interval
octave	+	second	=	ninth
	+	third	=	tenth
	+	fourth	=	eleventh
	+	fifth	=	twelfth
	+	sixth	=	thirteenth

NOTE: The intervals beyond the thirteenth exist in theory, but not in practice.

The quality of each compound interval is the same as the quality of the simple interval to which it is related—e.g. an octave plus a major second equals a major ninth, an octave plus a perfect fourth equals a perfect eleventh, etc. In every other way, compound intervals occur as melodic or harmonic intervals in the same way that simple intervals occur.

EXERCISE 1

Write compound intervals on the staff above the given notes.

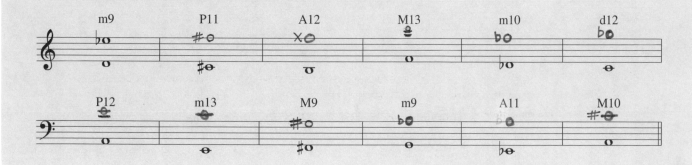

Extensions

Another term commonly used to describe compound intervals is *extended intervals*, or simply *extensions,* as these intervals extend beyond the octave. Extensions can also be added to the structure of a seventh chord to produce *extended chords*. Because two of the extensions—the tenth and the twelfth—are duplications of the third and the fifth that are already part of the basic chord structure, only the addition of the three remaining extensions, the *ninth*, *eleventh*, and *thirteenth*, actually result in extended chords.

Extended chords, taking their names from the extensions themselves, are called either *ninth chords*, *eleventh chords,* or *thirteenth chords.* We will look separately at how each individual extended chord is built, but all extended chords have certain things in common:

- **Extended chords are named by the largest unaltered interval present.** For example, if the chord contains a ninth and a thirteenth, it is called a thirteenth chord, with the presence of the smaller interval being assumed.
- **Adding extensions to a chord will not alter that chord's basic harmonic function.** For example, both D7 and D13 are V chords in the key of G; the presence of the thirteenth does not change the function, even though the chord sounds fuller and more dissonant.
- **Extended chords have the same qualities as the seventh chords on which they are based.** For instance, a *major* seventh chord with an added ninth is called a *major* ninth chord, a *dominant* chord with an added thirteenth is called a *dominant* thirteenth chord, etc. Extended chords may be seen as different shades of the same color.

Building Extended Chords

There are certain rules that must be followed in building extended chords that reflect the practical application of these chords. Each chord type is described separately.

Ninth Chords

Ninth chords are constructed by adding the interval of a *major ninth* to an existing seventh chord, regardless of its quality.

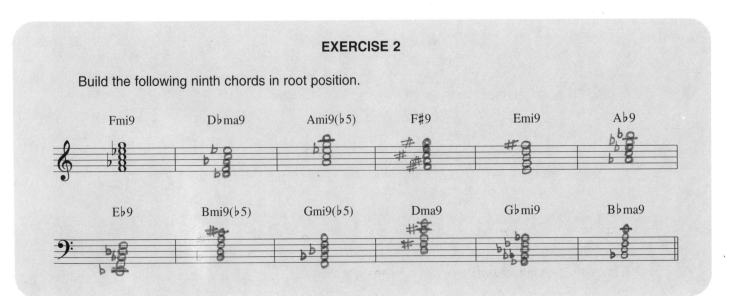

EXERCISE 2

Build the following ninth chords in root position.

Chapter 16

Eleventh Chords

Eleventh chords are created in theory by adding a perfect eleventh interval to an existing ninth chord. In practice, however, there are exceptions:

> **Major ninth and dominant ninth chords**: Because the perfect eleventh is a minor ninth interval above the major third degree of each of these chords, and because this interval is generally considered harsh or dissonant to the ear, *the eleventh is raised a half step* to reduce the dissonance. The name of the chord is then changed to reflect this alteration, becoming "ma9(♯11)" or "9(♯11)" to call attention to this change.

Fig. 2: raising the eleventh

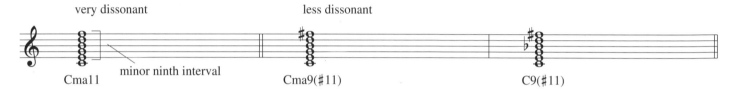

> **Minor ninth and minor ninth (♭5) chords**: Because these chords contain a *minor* third, the extreme dissonance is not present, so no alteration of the eleventh is required.

Fig. 3: minor eleventh and minor eleventh (♭5) chords

> **Replacing the third with the fourth**: If the third of the chord is replaced by the eleventh, it is not really an eleventh chord at all, but rather a "suspended fourth" chord (called "sus4" or simply "sus").

Fig. 4: replacing the third with the fourth

Summary of rules for chords containing elevenths:
1. Chords with major thirds use ♯11.
2. Chords with minor thirds use natural 11.
3. Chords with no thirds are actually "sus" chords.

NOTE: On chord charts, the symbol for the dominant eleventh chord, such as G11, is actually intended to represent a dominant ninth sus4 chord, or G9sus. The misuse of the dominant eleventh chord symbol is extremely common.

EXERCISE 3

Build the following eleventh and sus chords observing the rules above.

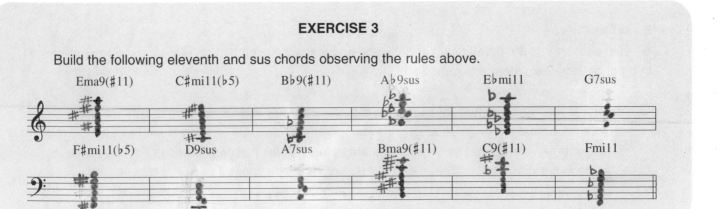

Thirteenth Chords

Complete thirteenth chords are built by adding the interval of a *major thirteenth* to an existing eleventh chord, taking into account the rules stated above. It is very important to note, however, that extended chords are usually voiced with fewer notes than those that are theoretically possible. The most common note to leave out of a thirteenth chord is the eleventh. If a thirteenth chord does contain an eleventh, and the eleventh is altered, the alteration must be written into the name of the chord, e.g., C13(#11).

Fig. 5: thirteenth chords

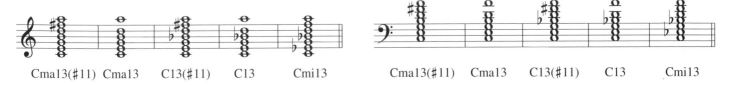

Cma13(#11) Cma13 C13(#11) C13 Cmi13   Cma13(#11) Cma13 C13(#11) C13 Cmi13

EXERCISE 4

Build the following thirteenth chords, taking into account the rules stated above.

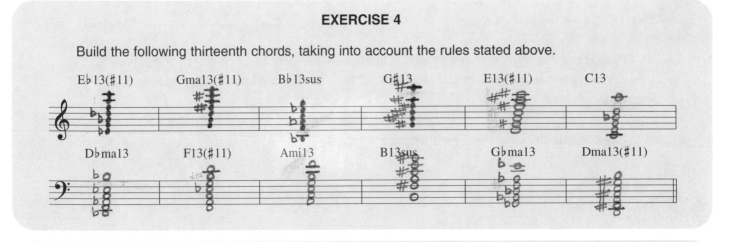

EXERCISE 5

Each of the following chords is written in root position. Figure out its proper name.

Other Chord Types

17

The one constant in popular music is change, and the harmony of popular music is changing just as constantly as any other element. Chord structure and movement in popular music is for the most part still surprisingly conservative, based on principles that have been around for hundreds of years, but new combinations of these underlying themes are continually being created, with the result that the theory of popular music—the explanations for why things work and what names to give them—is regularly evolving as well.

With respect to chords, continual change is reflected in the varieties of "new" or recombined sounds that evolve and the chord symbols that are used to represent them. A glance at any book of popular song charts will reveal a number of chord symbols that don't seem to fit into any of the categories that have been described so far. They are not triads, sevenths, extended, or altered chords, yet they are certainly common in even the simplest-sounding tunes. These other chord types can be grouped into three new categories: *variations on triads*, "*slash*" *chords* (non-root position, non-inverted chords), and *polychords*. In this chapter, we'll look at each of these categories of chords to learn their structure, application, and symbols.

Variations on Triads

All of the chords in this category are based on the sound of triads, yet they contain more or fewer tones than the standard root, third, and fifth. Because they contain no seventh, they are not truly extended chords, so they may generally be described as "triads with added color." New variations on these chords become popular from time to time, resulting in new chord names and symbols being invented to describe them. It takes a while for any one name or symbol to become universally recognized, and sometimes what emerges as the most popular name is not logically consistent with other chord names. The best approach to learning chord symbols is to maintain a logical system for naming chords while knowing the traditionally popular names as well, however inconsistent they may be.

Power Chords

"Power chord" is the typical name given to a chord containing only a root and perfect fifth degree, the third being omitted. (As with all chord voicings, the root and/or fifth may be doubled in different octaves.) The power comes from the neutral clarity of the perfect interval, without the emotional quality introduced by the presence of a major or minor third. Although it does not sound major or minor by itself, the quality of a power chord is implied by the overall tonality of the progression in which it is used. The symbol for a power chord is the letter name of the chord followed by the number 5, as in "C5".

Fig. 1: power chords

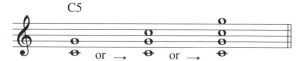

Suspended Fourth Chords

Commonly called "sus4" or simply "sus" chords, these are triads in which the fourth scale step replaces the third. Because the third is the strongest marker of chord quality, replacing the third with the fourth creates a feeling of being *suspended*, waiting for a resolution to return the chord to its original quality. Although the sus chord itself contains no third, its quality is implied by its resolution. Seventh or extended chords with a suspended fourth were discussed previously in Chapter 16. These are often misinterpreted as eleventh chords, although they have the same characteristics as a sus chord. The symbol for a sus chord is the letter name of the chord followed by "sus," as in "Csus."

Fig. 2: sus4 chords

Add2 Chords

"Add2" chords are major or minor triads, or power chords, with the addition of a major second interval above the root. These chords are often called "add9" chords, but since there is no seventh present in the chord, the use of the "2" is more accurate. (The octave in which the second is played is not relevant to the name of the chord.) The chord symbol for a major triad with an added second is the letter name of the chord followed by the number 2, as in "C2." A minor triad with an added second is "Cmi2," and a power chord with an added second is "C5/2."

Fig. 3: add2 chords

Sixth Chords

A major or minor triad with the addition of a major sixth interval above the root is called a *sixth chord*. The sixth interval may be voiced next to the fifth, in a different octave than the fifth, or replacing the fifth altogether. The chord symbol for a sixth chord is the letter name of the chord followed by the number 6, as in "C6" or "Cmi6."

Fig. 4: sixth chords

6/9 Chords

A major or minor triad with the addition of both a major sixth and a major ninth interval above the root is called a *6/9 chord*. (Although the 6/9 chord has no seventh, the use of the number "9" instead of the more logically consistent "2" is overwhelmingly traditional.) The chord symbol for a 6/9 chord is the letter name of the chord followed by 6/9, as in "C6/9" or "Cmi6/9."

Fig. 5: 6/9 chords

EXERCISE 1

Write these chords on the staff in root position.

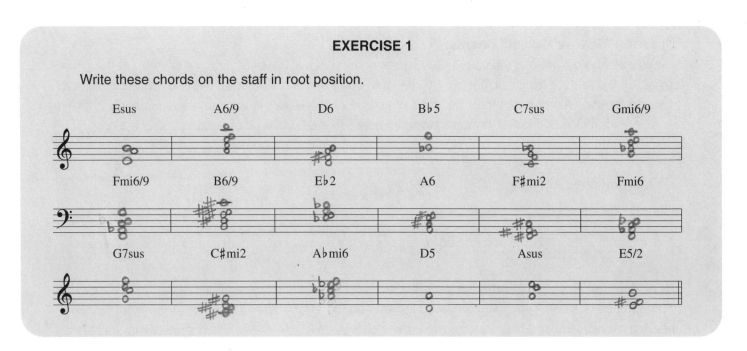

EXERCISE 2

Identify these chords. All are in root position.

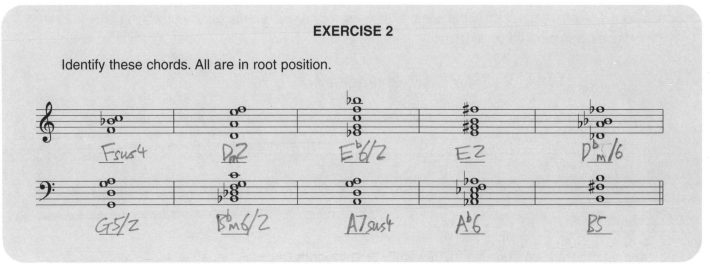

Slash Chords

The term "slash chord" is a simple way to describe any non-root position chord in which the chord quality and the bass note are divided in the chord symbol by a diagonal line, or slash. The chord is on the left, and the bass note is on the right. Slash chord symbols are a quick, simple method for representing complex sounds in a way that is immediately understandable by musicians of different styles and levels of education. Different instruments, depending on their roles and capabilities, interpret the sound of slash chords in different ways.

Fig. 6: slash chord symbols

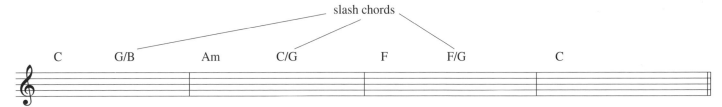

All slash chords fall into one of four categories:

1. Inverted Triads or Seventh Chords

In these chord symbols, the bass note (on the right) is either the third, fifth, or seventh of the chord quality (on the left). In traditional terms, these would be called *first inversion, second inversion,* or *third inversion* chords. (A chord with the root in the bass is in *root position,* which requires no slash.) Inverted chords are identified by looking at the relationship between the bass note and the chord. If the bass note is a chord tone, the chord is an inversion; if not, it belongs to one of the other categories.

Fig. 7: inverted chords

2. Root Position Seventh Chords Renamed

Sometimes a slash chord symbol actually represents a root position chord other than the one appearing in the symbol. For instance, writers will occasionally use slash chord symbols to simplify a keyboard part that involves a moving bass line, dividing the roles of the left and right hands by means of the slash. The resulting sound is the same either way it's named, so the choice of which name is best depends on the immediate circumstances.

EXERCISE 3

Name the root-position seventh chords that are equivalent in structure to these slash chords:

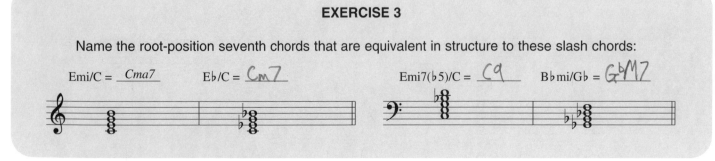

---

3. Incomplete Root Position Ninth, Eleventh, or Thirteenth Chords

Slash chord notation is often used to represent sounds that are more complex than triads but not as dissonant as full extended chords. By using a slash chord symbol with a triad on the left and the bass note on the right, the writer guides the player to a certain set of notes which, analyzed together, form an incomplete extended chord. If the normal root-position extended chord symbol were used, the additional notes that would normally be added might create a sound too complex for the setting. The slash chord symbol is the simplest, most direct way to describe the intended sound. The actual qualities and functions of these kinds of slash chords depends on how they are used in relation to the chords around them; often, the function is easier to identify by ear than by sight.

EXERCISE 4

Name the root-position extended chord or chords to which each of these slash chords is related. (One or more notes of the extended chord are omitted.)

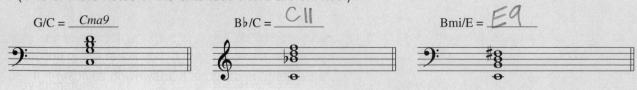

EXERCISE 5

In these two examples, the same slash chord is used in two different settings. Identify all of the chords, and analyze the quality and function of the slash chord in each example in relation to the chords around it.

4. A sound difficult to represent with a standard chord symbol

Sometimes a slash chord symbol is the only way to represent a chord that is too unusual and specific to the setting to be named with standard chord symbols. Attempting to name chords like these as root-position chords would result in symbols that are too complex or ambiguous to be interpreted consistently from one player or performance to the next.

EXERCISE 6

Name these chords with slash chord notation. Compare the resulting name with the equivalent standard root-position chord symbol.

Polychords

A *polychord* is a combination of two triads that together create a more complex sound. As with slash chords, polychord symbols are intended to quickly indicate the elements of the desired sound, with each part simple enough to be instantly identifiable. Polychords are favored by keyboard players, since the two sounds can be played easily using both hands. Guitar players tend to play them as slash chords, e.g., the upper triad played over the root of the lower triad. The chord symbol for a polychord consists of two different chord symbols placed one above the other and separated by a *horizontal* line (not to be confused with slash chords, which are separated by a diagonal line)

EXERCISE 7

Name the following polychord.

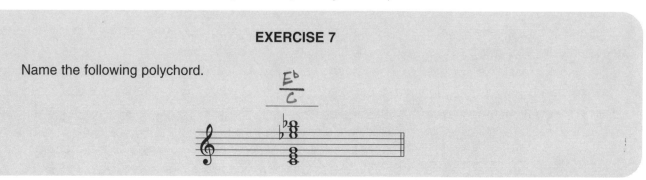

Part III: Variations
Melody and Harmony in the Real World

If your study of harmony and theory stopped with the diatonic system, you would find the world of popular music a very confusing and seemingly contradictory place. Chords appear to be thrown together almost at random, belonging to neither a major nor minor key for any length of time, with the wrong chord qualities on the wrong scale steps, and the melodies seeming to clash with the harmonies at every turn. However, underneath this apparent chaos, the diatonic system still functions, just in a more complex way. Systems are combined to create new systems, and chords and scales are still related but with a greater acceptance of dissonance.

Ironically, a close study of one of the greatest of popular songwriting groups, the Beatles, would reveal evidence of nearly every concept covered in the following section. Their natural talents and experience as songwriters gave them the ability to use such tricky devices as mixed harmonies and dissonant melodies in ways that didn't seem so abstract, and that's the underlying lesson—that complexity doesn't exist for its own sake, or to prove a theoretical point, but because it provides the right sound at the right time to express very human emotions.

Understanding the concepts explained in this section relies on understanding the previous structures of diatonic melody and harmony. Ideas are beginning to pile on top of one another, being supported by those below. You may find it necessary to review or do some exploring on your own to make some of these ideas and sounds really sink in, but once they do you'll begin to see and hear them as part of the everyday fabric of popular music in all its forms.

Modes
18

Variously referred to as the "Greek modes," "church modes," or "jazz modes," the modes of the major scale have been used for centuries as compositional tools and more recently as a popular source of melodic and harmonic variations for improvisers. The first step in being able to use modes effectively as a writer or player is to understand their structure. This chapter will show how each mode is built and offer you an overview of how modes are typically used in contemporary music.

Mode Construction

In modern popular music, melodies are rarely heard apart from harmony. That is, vocals and solos are heard over a background of chords, so that the structures of chords and scales are intertwined. To understand how modes are built, it is important to understand the chord/scale relationship in two ways: the relationship of individual chords and scales to each other, and the relationship of both chords and scales to a key.

First, look at the relationship of a C major seventh chord to the C major scale. The notes of the chord (the *chord tones*) are all present in the scale, and the scale also contains melodic notes (*scale tones*) between the chord tones that give the scale its smooth, stepwise structure.

Fig. 1: Cma7 and the C major scale

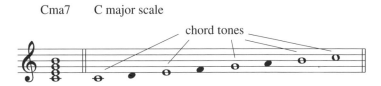

We know that the C major seventh chord is the I chord in the key of C major, so the root of the chord and the tonic of the scale are the same. We also know that the C major scale harmony contains a number of other chords and that, for each of these, the root of the chord is *not* the same as the tonic of the scale— Dmi7, for instance, is the IImi7 chord in the key of C major.

If the C major scale is played over a Dmi7 chord without any regard for this difference, the listener hears two subtly competing tone centers; that is, the melody is revolving around C while the harmony is based on D. However, if the tone center of the melody is shifted to D without changing the structure of the C major scale, the result is a scale that perfectly matches the sound of Dmi7 while keeping its relationship to the original key center intact. In other words, the notes of the C major scale are unchanged, but the note that receives the most emphasis is now D. By shifting the tone center, but maintaining the original structure, we have created a *mode* of the major scale.

Fig. 2: Dmi7 and its modal scale

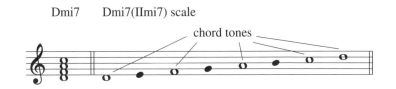

The same principle may be applied to each chord of the harmonized C major scale, resulting in a mode based on each scale tone. Like scale harmonies, the modes occur in the same order in every major key, so after learning their names and formulas in the key of C you can transfer that knowledge to all of the other keys.

Each mode has a unique name that sets it apart from other scales. These names originated in ancient Greece (hence the name *Greek modes*), were rediscovered in the Middle Ages, rearranged, and applied in sacred musical composition (hence the name *church modes*), and have been resurrected again by both modern classical and jazz musicians (hence the name *jazz modes*). While the original meaning of the name of each mode is obscure, modes are now commonly used by musicians all over the world.

When speaking or writing the name of a specific mode, use the letter name of the note on which it is built followed by the appropriate modal name, as in "D Dorian" or "F Lydian."

Fig. 3: the names of the modes

Ionian	related to Ima7 (the modal name for the major scale)
Dorian	related to IImi7
Phrygian	related to IIImi7
Lydian	related to IVma7
Mixolydian	related to V7
Aeolian	related to VImi7 (the modal name for natural minor)
Locrian	related to VIImi7(♭5)

EXERCISE 1

Build each of the seventh chords of the C harmonized scale on the staff below. On the left, build the chords vertically, in root position. On the right, draw the same notes horizontally, filling in the gaps between chord tones with the notes of the C major scale until you've created a one-octave modal scale. Finally, give each scale its proper modal name.

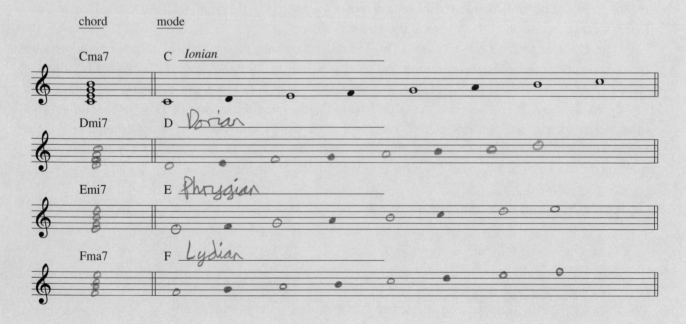

EXERCISE 1 (cont'd)

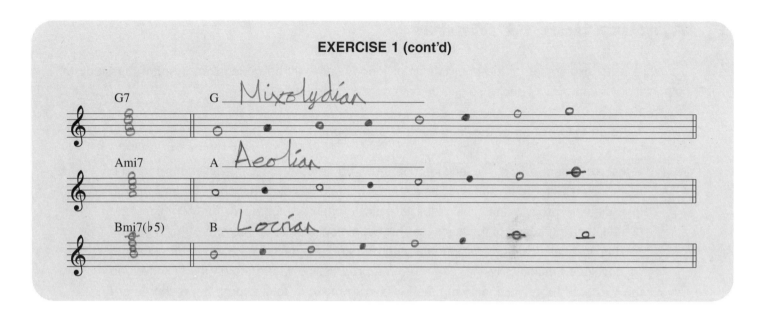

Once the names of the modes and the order in which they occur are memorized, it is possible to write any mode in any key using the following method:

Step 1: Determine the major scale degree on which the mode is built.
C Dorian, for example, is built on the second scale degree of B♭ major.

Step 2: Write the mode using the same key signature as the key from which it is derived.
If C Dorian is the second mode of B♭ major, it can be written using the key signature of B♭ major.

EXERCISE 2

Write out the following modes, with key signatures.

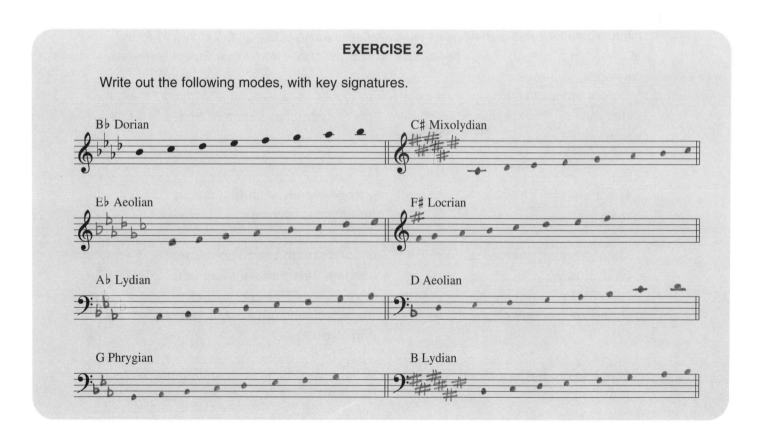

Application of Modes

While a full exploration of the applications of modes can only be undertaken through the study of composition or improvising, their use can be summarized in three basic ways:

1. As an elaboration of the "key center" approach

As explained previously, each mode may be related to a specific chord of the harmonized major scale and used as a source of melodies over that chord when it occurs in a diatonic progression. The result is a scale-oriented approach that combines the overall, unifying sound of the key center with a melodic focus on the root of each chord.

This application works best when a particular chord lasts long enough for the scale to be developed melodically—for example, in a progression where the harmony lingers on the V7 chord for a while, allowing the Mixolydian mode to take shape. If the chords are changing quickly, melodies based on individual modes simply don't have enough time to take on their separate identities; instead, basing melodies around the the actual chord tones or on the overall key center becomes a more effective approach.

2. As "sounds" outside of particular diatonic relationships

Chords are built in the same way regardless of where they are used in a scale harmony. Cmi7, for example, contains the same interval structure no matter whether it is used as the IImi7 chord in B♭, the IIImi7 chord in A♭, or the VImi7 chord in E♭. However, the modes built on those scale degrees, C Dorian, C Phrygian, and C Aeolian, all have different structures. If these three modes are taken out of their diatonic contexts and lined up side by side, they may be seen as three different scales usable over minor seventh chords. In a piece of music containing an extended solo over a Cmi7 chord, the modes could be intermingled to create interesting melodic effects, keeping in mind the fact that while they all "work" in theory, they may not always work in practice—something that only the ear can judge.

To use modes in this way, it is helpful to group them according to their overall quality rather than by their diatonic scale position. This results in four categories based on four distinct chord types:

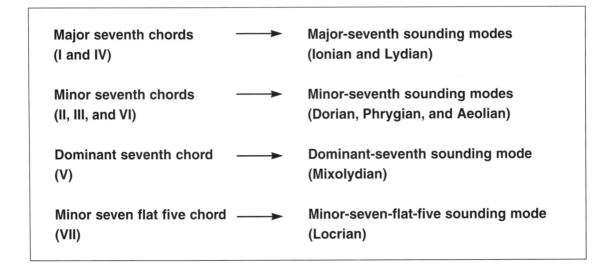

Major seventh chords (I and IV)	⟶	**Major-seventh sounding modes** (Ionian and Lydian)
Minor seventh chords (II, III, and VI)	⟶	**Minor-seventh sounding modes** (Dorian, Phrygian, and Aeolian)
Dominant seventh chord (V)	⟶	**Dominant-seventh sounding mode** (Mixolydian)
Minor seven flat five chord (VII)	⟶	**Minor-seven-flat-five sounding mode** (Locrian)

Chapter 18

EXERCISE 3

Build each mode based on the note C. Add sharps or flats as they occur.

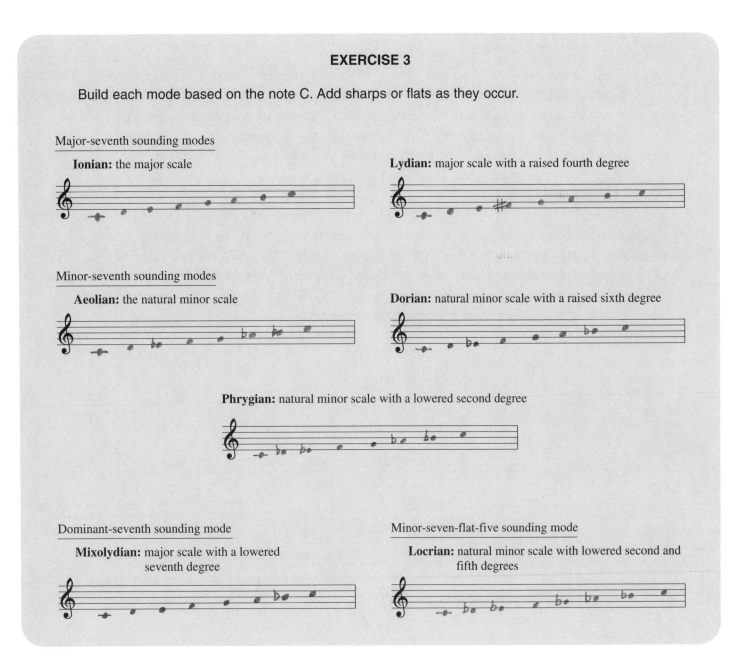

Major-seventh sounding modes

Ionian: the major scale

Lydian: major scale with a raised fourth degree

Minor-seventh sounding modes

Aeolian: the natural minor scale

Dorian: natural minor scale with a raised sixth degree

Phrygian: natural minor scale with a lowered second degree

Dominant-seventh sounding mode

Mixolydian: major scale with a lowered seventh degree

Minor-seven-flat-five sounding mode

Locrian: natural minor scale with lowered second and fifth degrees

Improvisors who take this approach of hearing the modes as "sounds" not directly related to a diatonic setting may use, for instance, the C Lydian mode over a C major seventh chord that is functioning as a I chord, with the result that the melody contains a raised fourth, creating a surprising, and hopefully interesting, variation in an otherwise standard phrase.

Another extremely common application of this approach is in blues, where all of the chords are typically dominant seventh chords, and the Mixolydian scale of each chord, regarded as the basic dominant seventh scale, can be used as a source of improvisation regardless of the particular function of that chord in the key.

A further extension of this idea is the use of a mode as a sound not directly related to the chord structure itself. For example, when C Phrygian, a minor-sounding mode, is applied over a C major triad, the resulting melody resembles Spanish flamenco music.

3. As a basis for altered scales

By combining or altering the structures of the modes themselves, new melodic combinations can be developed. For example, a major scale with a raised fourth (derived from Lydian) combined with the flatted seventh (derived from Mixolydian) produces a scale known as "Lydian dominant" or "Lydian flat seven," which is then commonly used as a twist on the standard dominant seventh scale sound. Using modes in this way depends on a thorough understanding of their basic structure so that the variations may be clearly seen and heard.

Modes have been the subject of a great many books on composition and improvisation, and writers and players have devoted a great deal of study to their use over the years. Modes may also be derived from the harmonies of other scales, although these subjects lie beyond the scope of this book. The complexity of modes lies not so much in their structure but in their various applications; this chapter is just an introduction to a fascinating and wide-ranging subject.

19 Variations in Minor Harmony

Our original discussion of harmony in minor keys explained the purely diatonic relationships between minor scales and chord progressions. However, this basic theory does not fully explain the reality of how minor scales and harmonies are applied in practice. There are several important and common variations that occur within the minor diatonic system, and this chapter and the next will explain them as we continue to close the gap between theory and reality.

The Leading Tone and the V7 Chord

One of the things you might notice when you listen closely to the harmony of a typical "real world" minor-key tune is that the Vmi chord is more than likely a *major* triad or *dominant seventh* chord, rather than being a minor triad or minor seventh chord as the natural minor scale harmony would lead you to expect. The reason for this apparent inconsistency is due to the different melodic structures of major and minor scales and the effect that they have on listeners. To learn why this is, we'll begin by reviewing the structure of the natural minor scale.

EXERCISE 1

On the staff, write a C natural minor scale, and build the diatonic triads on the first, fourth, and fifth degrees.

In a harmonized natural minor scale, the qualities of the Imi, IVmi, and Vmi triads are all minor. This consistency in the qualities of the three main chords is part of what gives the minor key its characteristic color, just as the major quality of the I, IV, and V triads in the harmonized major scale form an essential part of that sound.

From a traditional composer's view, however, the natural minor scale contains a basic flaw that is reflected in both its diatonic melodies and harmonies. The problem is that the whole step between the seventh and eighth degrees of the minor scale fails to lead the melody into the tonic with the same degree of pull that is created by the half step in that same position within the major scale. The gravitational force of the half step is a large factor in establishing the strong sense of tonality in a major key, and by comparison the natural minor scale sounds less conclusive. The solution devised by composers centuries ago was to duplicate that gravitational force in minor keys by altering the minor scale, raising the seventh degree a half step and thereby closing the gap with the tonic. Based on its tendency to lead the melody to resolution, the name given to the raised seventh in both major and minor keys is the *leading tone*.

Fig. 1: C natural minor with raised seventh degree

leading tone

EXERCISE 2

On the staff, write a C minor scale with a leading tone. Build the triads on the first, fourth, and fifth degrees, including the same alteration in the chord structure.

The alteration of the scale to create a leading tone has an effect on the quality of the V triad as well, changing the triad from minor to major. In major keys, the strength of the V–I chord progression comes largely from the pull of the leading tone (which is the major third degree of the V triad) to the root of the I chord. With the creation of a leading tone in the minor scale, the same strength exists in the V–Imi progression in minor keys.

Add the seventh chord degree to the V major triad in Exercise 1, and see what chord quality results. The addition of the seventh to the triad creates a dominant seventh chord, resulting in a V7–Imi resolution, which again is stronger than the diatonic Vmi7–Imi resolution. Because of the effect on the scale harmony that results from raising the seventh degree of the minor scale, this altered scale is called *harmonic minor.* Later in this book we will return to the harmonic minor scale to look more closely at its structure and relationship with other minor scales.

In the years since the evolution of the leading tone and the V7 chord in minor keys, the relationship between harmony and melody has undergone significant changes. Alterations in one are no longer always directly reflected in the other. For example, in modern styles such as blues and rock, a V7 chord containing a leading tone may be used simultaneously with an unaltered seventh in the melody. What was once regarded as unacceptable dissonance is now taken for granted. The educated musician understands the rules even while breaking them.

The Diminished Seventh Chord

Raising the seventh degree of the minor scale affects the diatonic scale harmony of a minor key in more than one way. Another result is that the root of the ♭VII7 chord is raised by a half step, changing both the name of the chord and its quality.

EXERCISE 3

Write a C harmonic minor scale on the staff, then build a diatonic seventh chord on the raised seventh degree of the scale.

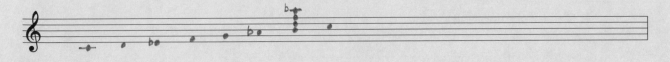

The resulting chord is similar to the VII chord in the harmonized major scale, but differs in one important way. Rather than forming a Bmi7(♭5) chord, harmonizing the seventh degree of the harmonic minor scale forms a complete *diminished seventh chord*, or B°7. Both chords are based on a diminished triad, differing in the seventh degree only. (The mi7(♭5) chord is sometimes called a "half diminished chord" to highlight the difference.)

Like the V7 chord, the VII°7 chord contains a leading tone and has a strong pull toward the tonic. In traditional classical harmony, the VII°7 is nearly always used as the VII° chord in minor keys. In modern popular harmony, though, it is quite common to continue to use the ♭VII major triad or dominant seventh chord even when the V7 is present in the same progression, because in some settings the VII°7 is considered too complex and dissonant compared to the other triads or seventh chords.

The diminished seventh chord is a different basic chord type than the other chords in the harmonized diatonic major and minor scales. Its formula is as follows:

Fig. 2: the diminished seventh chord

Interval formula: root, minor third, diminished fifth, diminished seventh

The presence of the diminished seventh chord degree, one half step smaller than a minor seventh, means that occasionally the use of a double flat (♭♭) is required to correctly identify the seventh.

EXERCISE 4

Write the diminished seventh chords on the staff, using double flat signs where necessary.

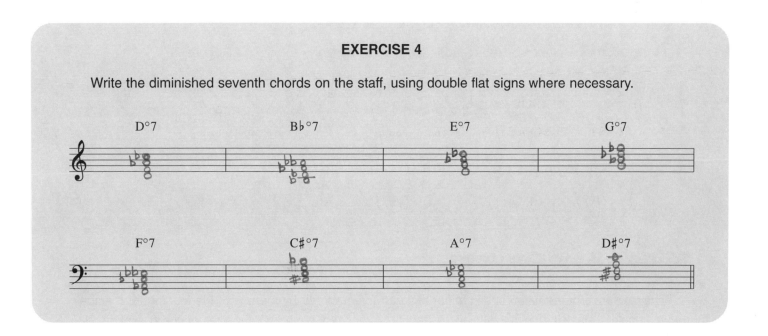

The Minor/Major Seventh Chord

The use of the leading tone in minor keys has one other common, though indirect, effect on the harmony. This is the creation of the *minor/major seventh chord*, which is another distinct chord quality apart from the others.

Fig. 3: the minor/major seventh chord

Interval formula: root, minor third, perfect fifth, major seventh

Although this chord is derived from the harmony of the harmonic minor scale, where it functions as a Imi chord, it is too dissonant to be generally applied as a true tonic chord. Instead, it is almost always used in a very specific context within both minor and major keys as a colorful melodic embellishment on the sound of a minor chord, whether or not it is functioning as a Imi chord.

Fig. 4: typical use of the minor/major seventh chord

EXERCISE 5

Write the minor/major seventh chords on the staff above the roots, and label each.

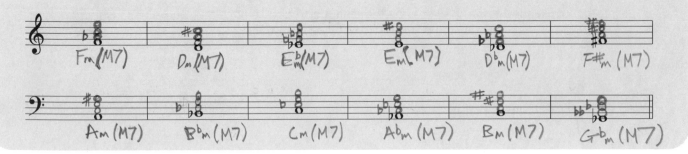

Minor Key Centers

The presence of the variations in minor key harmony created by the use of the leading tone actually make it easier, rather than more difficult, to identify key centers based on analyses of chord relationships. In major key centers, the basic rule for locating the tonic was to find the dominant chord, and in minor keys the same rule now usually applies. The diminished seventh chord has functions other than as a VII chord which will be explored later, but as a diatonic chord its tendency to resolve upward is also an indicator of the tonic.

EXERCISE 6

Analyze the progressions below to locate the key, and identify the function of each chord within its minor key center.

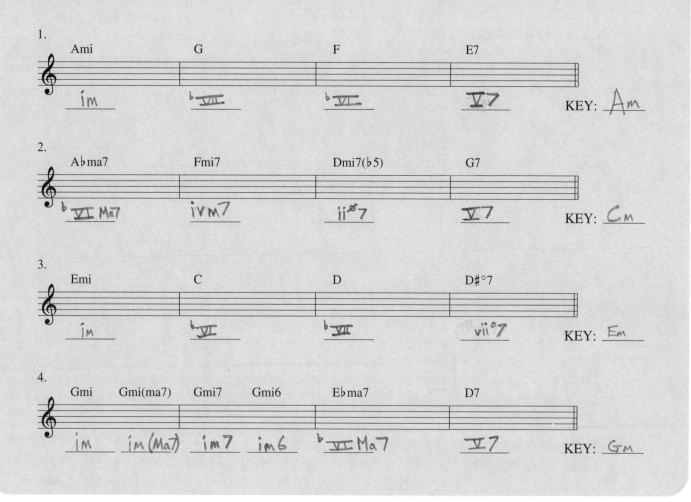

Combining Major and Minor Key Centers

It is very common for major and minor key centers to both exist in the same piece of music, with the key center temporarily shifting from one to the other. The presence of a V7–I progression is still the best indicator of the key, even if it is only temporary. Often, a chord may seem on paper to have more than one function, and in this case, the ear must be the judge as to what key is implied. For example, the minor7(♭5) chord functions both as a VII chord in major keys and a II chord in minor keys. This is confusing to the eye, but the ear will nearly always hear this chord as belonging to the minor tonality.

A useful analysis of chord progressions has to be based on what is heard, since the reason for analysis in the first place is to learn to understand and manipulate sound. The more experience a musician has playing different types of music, the more useful any analysis will be in creating a practical result. Through ear training, you can learn to hear what you see on paper. Until this skill is developed, always play the examples to confirm what your eyes are telling you.

EXERCISE 7

The progressions below contain mixed major and minor key centers. Write the Roman numeral function below each chord, and indicate the key centers in brackets above each group of chords.

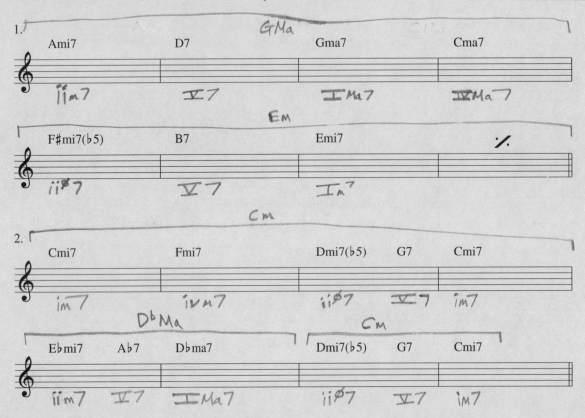

In the next example, containing two key centers, only triads are used. The V–I relationship is still the strongest indicator of key, but because the V chord is a major triad, it is necessary to look at the interval relationships between the chord roots to accurately locate the tonic. In progressions of this type, the ear can usually locate the tonic more quickly than the eye.

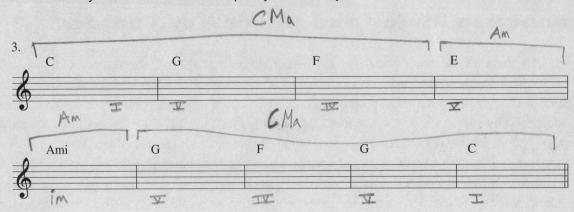

20 Variations in Minor Melody

In the last chapter, we looked at several ways in which an alteration in the structure of the minor scale—raising the seventh degree—is reflected in the qualities of the chords related to that scale. In this chapter, we'll look more closely at this and the other common melodic variations in the minor scale, along with some other related harmonic changes.

The Harmonic Minor Scale

As discussed in the previous chapter, the alteration of the natural minor scale to include a leading tone also has the effect of increasing the sense of movement in minor-key chord progressions. Because of the relationship between the scale structure and the harmony, the minor scale that includes this alteration is called the *harmonic minor scale*. The harmonic minor scale does not have its own key signature. The raised seventh is treated as a variation to the normal natural minor key signature, and whenever the alteration occurs in a melody, it is indicated by an accidental.

Fig. 1: the A harmonic minor scale

EXERCISE 1

Build each of the following harmonic minor scales by writing the appropriate minor key signature on the staff, filling in the scale steps, and indicating the raised seventh with an accidental.

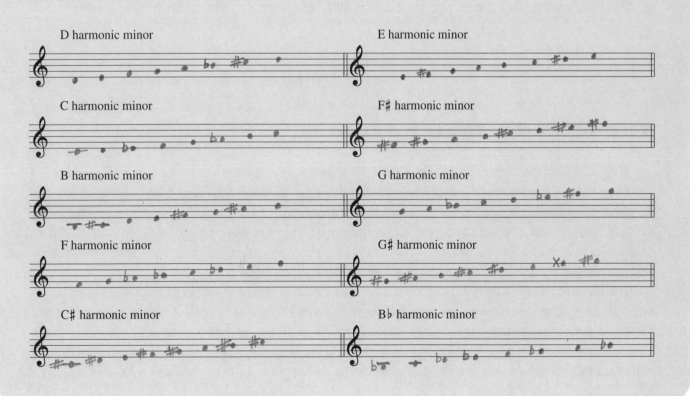

When we looked at the effect of the raised seventh on the diatonic harmony of the minor scale, we saw that it mainly creates a stronger feeling of resolution from the V to the Imi chord. The other chords in the natural minor scale harmony are mostly left unchanged, with the exception of the occasional VII°7 or Imi(ma7) chord. The result is that since the natural minor scale fits perfectly well over all of the diatonic chords except V7, it is still treated as the basic key center scale for improvisation, and the harmonic minor variation is used in the melody only together with the V7 chord in the harmony. Therefore, the harmonic minor scale may be seen as a temporary coloration of the natural minor sound rather than as an entirely different scale.

The chord progression below is bracketed to show a typical application of the harmonic minor scale when improvising over a minor-key chord progression. Notice that the A harmonic minor scale is applied only over the E7 chord; otherwise, the progression is diatonic to the A natural minor scale.

Fig. 2: application of the harmonic minor scale

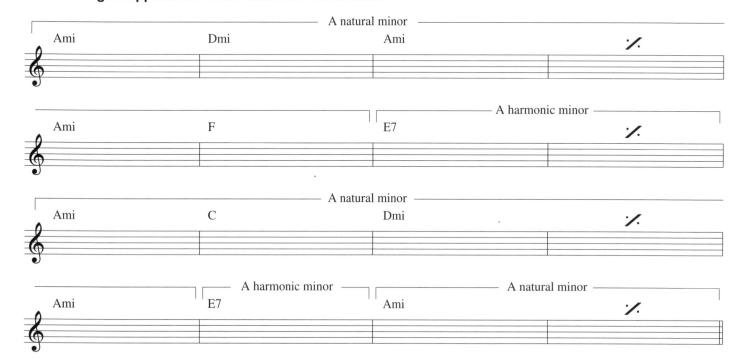

The Melodic Minor Scale

While the harmonic minor scale "fixes" one perceived flaw in the natural minor scale (i.e. the lack of a leading tone), it creates yet another one—an increased gap between the minor sixth and major seventh degrees of the scale. Raising the seventh makes this an interval of 1 1/2 steps. When the harmonic minor scale is played in its entirety, it sounds somewhat exotic from the viewpoint of Western music, and its usefulness therefore becomes limited in this context. In response to this problem, the *melodic minor scale* was created to "fix" the harmonic minor scale while retaining its leading tone.

The melodic minor scale is created by raising both the sixth and seventh degrees of the natural minor scale. Raising the sixth closes the gap between the minor sixth and major seventh degrees of the harmonic minor scale, making the upper structure of the scale as "melodic" as that of the major scale. Like the harmonic minor scale, the melodic minor scale is commonly seen as an alteration of the natural minor scale, and accidentals are used to indicate the raised sixth and seventh within the natural minor key signature.

Fig. 3: the A melodic minor scale

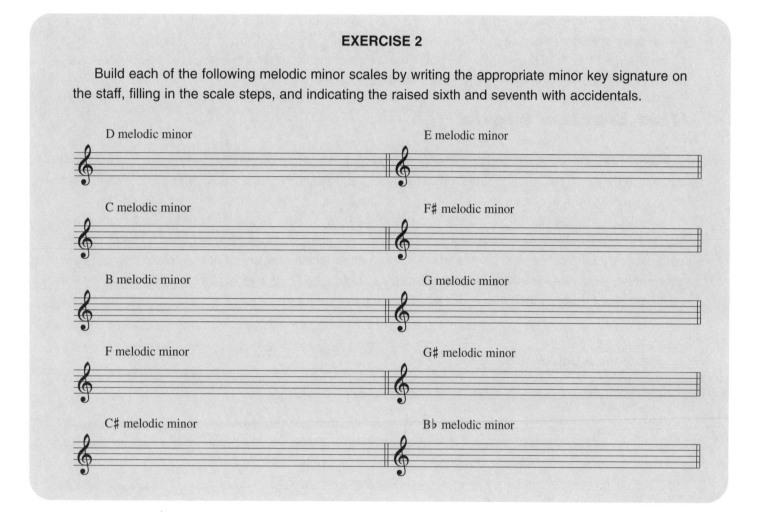

In traditional music theory, the melodic minor scale is actually constructed differently depending on whether the melody is ascending or descending. This is because the raised tones create an upward pull toward the octave in an ascending melody, while the natural minor scale with its lowered sixth and seventh creates more of a pull toward the fifth scale degree, another important melodic tone, in a descending melody. Therefore, the traditional melodic minor scale has an ascending structure with raised tones and a different descending structure that is identical to the natural minor scale.

Fig. 4: the traditional melodic minor scale

In contemporary usage, however, the melodic minor scale is built the same way ascending and descending, a structure sometimes known as "jazz melodic minor." It is primarily used as a scale for improvisation in jazz-related styles and is frequently superimposed over chords in various ways far different from its traditional melodic usage. These applications will be covered in a later chapter.

In popular music, the melodic minor scale is rarely used as a complete scale sound. The raised seventh is more typically treated as part of the harmonic minor scale (or simply as a temporary alteration of the natural minor scale, as explained above). The raised sixth, while it does close the gap between the minor sixth and the major seventh, clashes with the other chords of the natural minor scale, which typically form the bulk of the harmony of popular songs in minor keys. The raised sixth is more commonly heard in the context of the next minor scale, the *Dorian mode.*

The Dorian Mode

The Dorian mode and its construction have already been discussed in the chapter on modes. In the context of minor scales, though, the Dorian mode is frequently used as a key-center scale with its own scale harmony, and, in certain styles such as rock, the Dorian mode is as common as natural minor.

The Dorian mode can be constructed in one of two ways. First, it can be built by applying the key signature of the parent major scale, as described in the chapter on modes. Second, the Dorian mode can be created by raising the sixth degree of the natural minor scale built on the same tonic. The first view shows the overall diatonic relationship of the modes, but the second view is more helpful in hearing the relationship of Dorian to the other minor scales, and it is the one used here.

Fig. 5: the A Dorian mode

In the harmonic minor scale, the raised seventh degree changes the quality of the V chord from minor to major. In the Dorian scale, raising the sixth degree of the natural minor scale has the same effect on the IV chord, changing the quality of that chord from a minor triad to a major triad. Dorian scale harmony also differs from natural minor scale harmony in other ways. The most important difference is that the quality of the II chord in Dorian harmony is minor rather than diminished, making it less dissonant and therefore more useful in chord progressions based mainly on major and minor triads.

Fig. 6: Dorian scale harmony

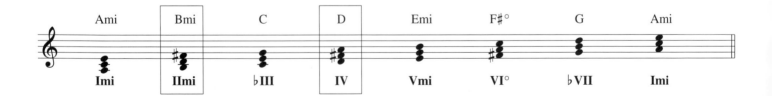

The addition of sevenths to the scale harmony gives the IV chord a dominant seventh quality and the IImi chord a minor seventh quality.

Fig. 7: the Dorian mode harmonized in sevenths

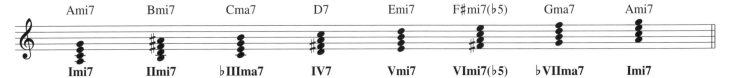

The variations that occur in minor scale harmony between the natural minor scale and other minor scales make the task of identifying key centers by sight somewhat more difficult. For example, a dominant seventh chord may not always be a V chord, and a V chord may not always be a dominant seventh chord. More than ever, the ability to play or sing the root progression and identify the resolutions by sound is important. Especially in modal progressions, the sound of the chords may lead you to a much different idea of where the key center is than their appearance on paper.

EXERCISE 3

Identify the key center of the following progression, and write the function of each chord below the staff.

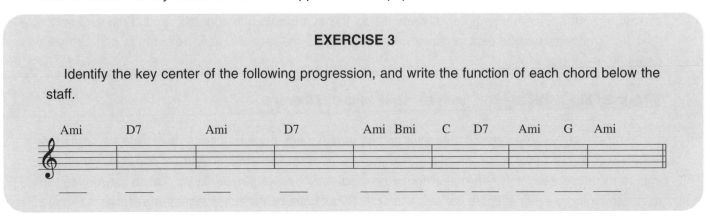

Remembering all of the minor scale variations can be confusing if they are thought of as completely separate sounds. Although the differences are important, the scales are actually much more alike than not. By arranging them side by side and comparing them to the natural minor scale, it is easy to see how much they all have in common even while the differences are highlighted.

Fig. 8: comparing the minor scales

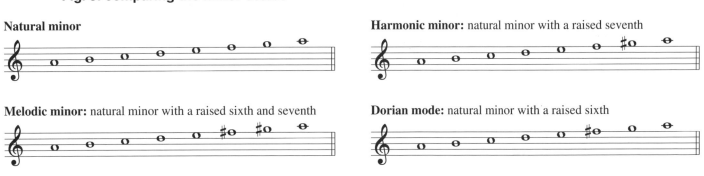

The first five notes of each scale are identical, with the variations occuring only in the sixth and seventh degrees. This type of comparison is especially useful when applying these scales to an instrument, as the natural minor scale pattern may be memorized and then altered slightly to create any of the other scales. In practice, the variations of the sixth and seventh are often used in different combinations depending on the harmony of the moment, so seeing and hearing them as versions of a single minor tonality reflects the reality in which they function.

Modal Interchange
21

The diatonic major and minor systems go a long way toward describing the sounds that are typical of popular music, but there are many instances in which chord progressions do not seem to fit the rules of any one key. Often a progression will be obviously based around a major or minor tonic chord but will also include other chords that do not belong to the scale harmony of the tonic. The general term that describes harmony that is nondiatonic is *chromatic harmony,* that is, harmony that includes notes that are not found in the diatonic scale. Chromatic harmony is not necessarily dissonant. In fact, some very popular styles of music, such as blues and rock, actually depend on chromatic harmony for their sound.

It is interesting to note that some of the chord progressions that are simplest to hear and play require considerable theoretical explanation. This is because the diatonic systems were developed before the impact of non-Western styles, such as blues, introduced sounds to modern music that were outside the rules of classical harmony. In an effort to expand these rules, various theories have been developed to explain how chromatic harmony functions and how it may be quickly recognized and labeled. Over the next few chapters, we will explore several of the theories that are the most relevant to the everyday harmony of popular music.

Parallel Major and Minor Keys

As previously discussed, *relative* major and minor keys are those that share the same key signature but have different tonic notes, such as C major and A minor, or E major and C♯ minor. Another very important relationship between major and minor scales is that of *parallel* keys. These are defined as major and minor keys that share the same tonic note but have different key signatures, such as C major and C minor, or A major and A minor. Although parallel major and minor scales sound quite different from each other, the fact that they are centered around the same tonic gives them a strong feeling of connection just the same.

EXERCISE 1

On the first staff, write the C major scale and its parallel minor. On the second, write the A minor scale and its parallel major. (Write the sharps and flats before each note as needed.)

Modal Interchange

The two basic tonal qualities in traditional Western European music are major and minor. In classical music theory, these two tonalities, including the diatonic major and minor scales and their resulting harmonies, are referred to as *modes,* i.e., as the "major mode" and the "minor mode." (This is the usual classical meaning for the word "modes," as opposed to the Greek modes, which have been described earlier.)

Up to this point, we have learned and applied the major and minor modes as completely separate systems, each based on its own tonal center. A great many chord progressions may be analyzed as belonging to one mode or the other, but an equally great number cannot be clearly explained in this way. For example, it is impossible to analyze the progression below as belonging to any one major or minor key.

Fig. 1: mixed-mode progression

The progression appears to be centered around C major, as it begins and ends on that chord. The B♭ major and E♭ major chords, however, clearly do not belong to the scale harmony of C major, nor does C major belong to their scale harmonies. If the progression is played, there is no doubt that it is very ordinary-sounding and not at all dissonant or awkward to the ear. How, then, can these apparently unrelated chords be explained as "belonging" to the tonality of C major when they obviously don't fit within the C major diatonic system? The answer lies in the concept known as *modal interchange*. This explains chord progressions like the one above as a product of mixing, or interchanging, the scale harmonies of parallel major and minor modes.

EXERCISE 2

Write the harmonized C major scale in triads, and name each chord.

Write the harmonized C minor scale in triads, and name each chord.

Notice that the E♭ and B♭ chords which defied explanation as part of the C major system do in fact belong to the C *minor* system. The basic concept of modal interchange is that the strength of the relationship of both modes to a single tonic allows the scale harmonies to be interchanged in this way. Because C major is the tonic chord, the E♭ and B♭ are analyzed as chords that have been "borrowed" from C minor, adding color to the original tonality without actually changing the tone center. Given this analysis, the scale function of each chord is numbered as follows:

Fig. 2: mixed-mode progression analyzed

C major is the "original" mode of the progression, so the other chords are numbered as alterations. Comparing the major and minor scale harmonies in this way, the numbering of the scale steps for the entire key is as follows:

Fig. 3: analysis of "borrowed" parallel minor chords

Scale Step	I	IImi	IIImi	IV	V	VImi	VII°
Major Mode	C	Dmi	Emi	F	G	Ami	B°
Parallel Minor	Cmi	D°	E♭	Fmi	Gmi	A♭	B♭
Modal Interchange Analysis	**Imi**	**II°**	**♭III**	**IVmi**	**Vmi**	**♭VI**	**♭VII**

EXERCISE 3

Analyze the progression to find which chords belong to the key of A major and which belong to the parallel minor. Write the chord functions below the staff.

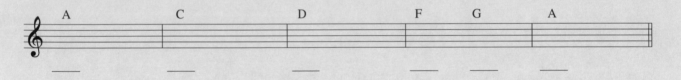

In the greatest number of cases, modal interchange occurs when the tonic chord is major and borrowing is done from the parallel minor. Sometimes, though, the process works the other way as well, when the tonic chord is minor, and chords are borrowed from the parallel major.

EXERCISE 4

Analyze the progression to identify which chords belong to the key of C minor and which belong to the parallel major.

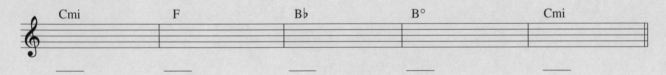

To number the borrowed major-scale chords, they are labeled as alterations of the original minor-scale harmony.

Fig. 4: analysis of "borrowed" parallel major chords

Scale Step	Imi	II°	♭III	IVmi	Vmi	♭VI	♭VII
Minor Mode	Cmi	D°	E♭	Fmi	Gmi	A♭	B♭
Parallel Minor	C	Dmi	Emi	F	G	Ami	B°
Modal Interchange Analysis	**I**	**IImi**	**♮IIImi**	**IV**	**V**	**♮VImi**	**♮VII°**

Notice that two of the borrowed parallel major chords, IImi and IV, are identical to chords that were previously identified as belonging to the scale harmony of the Dorian mode. Also, the V and raised VII° have already appeared as chords related to the harmonic minor scale. It is a fact that there is often more than one way to explain harmonic relationships, so the important thing is to find the best explanation for the required purpose. For a composer, modal interchange is a valuable tool because it offers a way of finding new sounds within a familiar system. For an improvisor, relating chords to a specific scale is valuable because it quickly provides a set of good-sounding notes without awkward trial-and-error experimentation. Each explanation is valuable in its own way without contradicting the other. Musicians are known to engage in heated debate over which particular system is best for explaining the most things, but exposure to various ways of analyzing chord progressions ultimately creates greater depth of understanding and allows each musician to synthesize the personal system that best serves his or her own purpose.

EXERCISE 5

Each of the following four progressions contains examples of modal interchange. First, determine whether the tonic chord is major or minor. Then analyze the function of each chord, writing the scale step number below the staff.

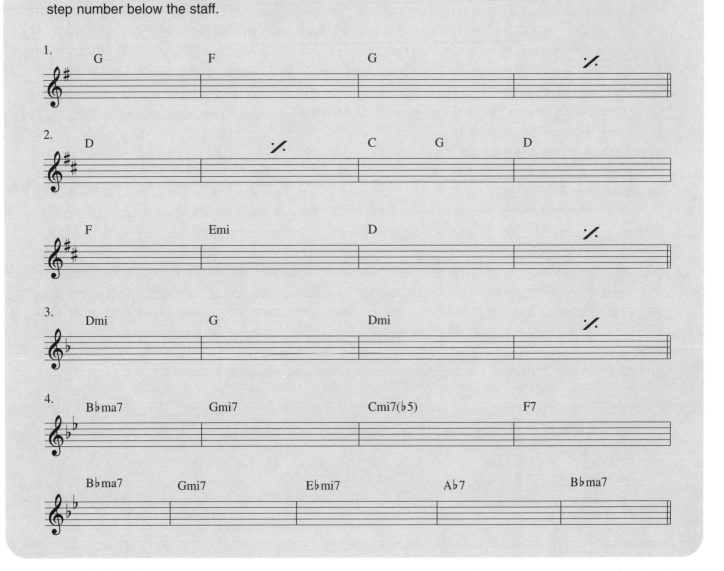

Secondary Dominants

The concept of modal interchange goes a long way toward explaining relationships between nondiatonic chords that belong to a single tonality. This chapter, however, will concentrate on another category of chords that fits the same description but cannot be explained by means of modal interchange.

EXERCISE 1

Analyze the progression below, identifying the function of each chord.

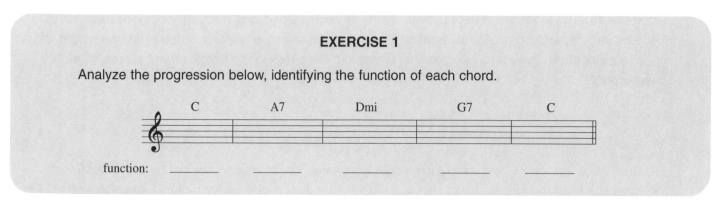

function: _____ _____ _____ _____ _____

Based on analyses of chord progressions up to this point, it would appear that there are two keys in this progression, because there are two different dominant seventh chords; in diatonic harmony, the dominant seventh chord is the strongest clue pointing to the key center, because it is always a V chord in major keys, and nearly always in minor keys. According to this analysis, in this progression the key of C major is indicated by the G7 chord, and the key of D minor is indicated by the A7 chord. However, the Dmi chord is also the IImi chord in the key of C. Does the A7 chord actually represent a change of key or is there another explanation?

As usual, listening to the progression will unlock secrets that the eye may not see. It will be apparent to the ear that the tone center of the entire progression is C, with the A7 sounding like a variation on the diatonic VImi chord, Ami, and the Dmi chord sounding in fact like a IImi chord. The change in the quality of the A chord increases the sense of anticipation that D minor is about to arrive, but does not signal the presence of a new key. The A7 chord is an example of a *secondary dominant.*

Although the secondary dominant seems to break the rule that dominant seventh chords function as V chords, the rule actually still applies. A secondary dominant chord still functions as a V chord, but *it is the V of a chord other than I.* In the example above, A7 is the V7 of IImi. This analysis shows that C is still considered to be the tonic, G7 is the "primary" dominant of the key of C, and the function of A7 is to present the Dmi chord in a more dramatic way than would be accomplished by the diatonic VImi chord, Ami. The function of A7 is written as "V7/II" (spoken as "five seven of two"), making its role in the progression clear. Therefore, the complete analysis of the progression is as follows:

Fig. 1: analysis of the function of the secondary dominant

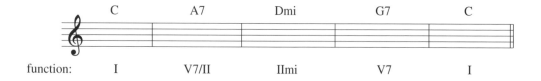

function: I   V7/II   IImi   V7   I

NOTE: The description of A7 as V7/II explains its function in the progression, which is the purpose of harmonic analysis. However, since the root, A, is the sixth degree of the C major scale, A7 sounds to the ear simply like VI7; that is, its function does not become apparent until the next chord sounds and the secondary dominant relationship is established. In everyday musical conversation, it is very common for this chord to be described as VI7, as in, "The progression goes from I to VI dominant to II–V–I." This description is much quicker for the purpose of describing and remembering what chords are to be played than saying, "Go from I to the V7 of ii minor," etc. Even while VI7 is the quickest description, to understand harmony it is necessary to be aware of the intended function of chords, which makes V7/II the best analysis. Know the difference between description and analysis, and use the best name for the situation.

Types of Secondary Dominants

Secondary dominants may occur in both major and minor keys. The overall rule is this:

> Any diatonic chord may be preceded by its secondary dominant except
> the VII° chord in major and the II° chord in minor.

The exclusion of the VII° and II° chords is due to the fact that these chords are each based on a diminished triad, which is considered too dissonant to function even temporarily as a point of resolution. As the role of the secondary dominant is to increase the sense of anticipation for the coming chord, the chord of resolution must be able to stand on its own, or the overall flow of the progression is broken.

There are a limited number of possible secondary dominants; with practice, they become easy to spot by eye.

EXERCISE 2

Each of the following examples in the key of C major or C minor contains one or more secondary dominants. Analyze the progressions, and write down the function of each chord using the same type of Roman numeral symbols as shown above, e.g., "V7/VI," "V7/IV," etc.

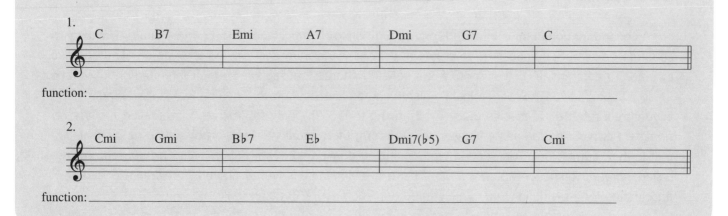

1.

C   B7   Emi   A7   Dmi   G7   C

function: _____

2.

Cmi   Gmi   Bb7   Eb   Dmi7(b5)   G7   Cmi

function: _____

EXERCISE 2 (cont'd)

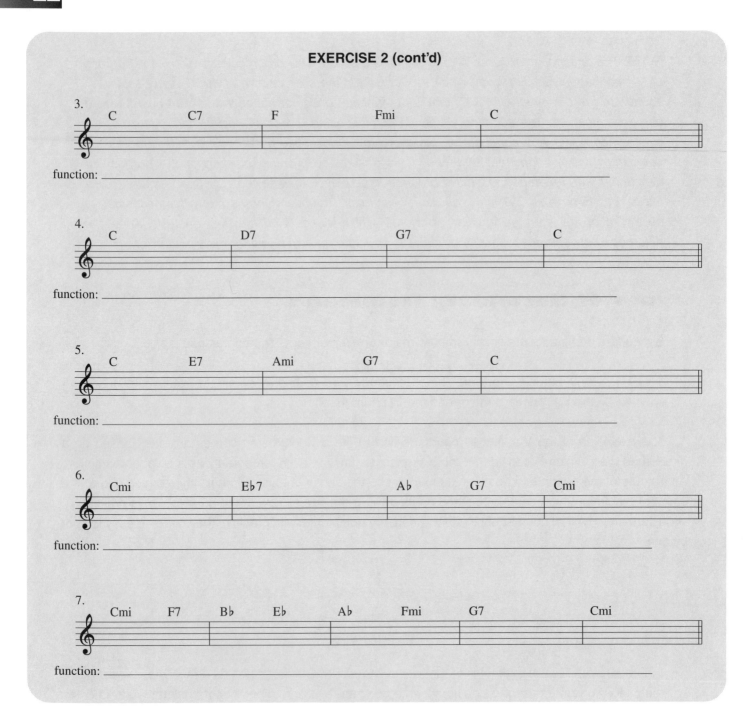

3.

C   C7   F   Fmi   C

function: _____

4.

C   D7   G7   C

function: _____

5.

C   E7   Ami   G7   C

function: _____

6.

Cmi   Eb7   Ab   G7   Cmi

function: _____

7.

Cmi   F7   Bb   Eb   Ab   Fmi   G7   Cmi

function: _____

Variations on Secondary Dominants

A secondary dominant is intended to create a sense of anticipation for a certain chord. However, a common device of composers is to create anticipation and then deceive the listener, creating surprise instead. To differentiate between dominant seventh chords that resolve to their intended chord versus those that don't, two types of dominant seventh chords are recognized. The first type, including dominant seventh chords that do resolve (such as V7 going to I, V7/II going to IImi, etc.), are called *functioning dominant chords*. As the name implies, they perform their traditional function of setting up a resolution that is then carried out. The second type, including dominant seventh chords that *do not* resolve, are called *nonfunctioning dominant chords*. These are dominant seventh chords that create a sense of anticipation for a resolution that is *not* carried out, such as V7/VI going to IV, etc.

Since the dominant seventh chord is used for the same purpose either way, i.e. creating a sense of expectation, the analysis remains the same whether it is functioning or nonfunctioning.

EXERCISE 3

Analyze the first four progressions in the key of C major. They include examples of modal interchange as well as functioning and nonfunctioning secondary dominants. Analyze the last progression in the key of A major.

Altered Chords

23

Our discussion of chromatic harmony has led us to two ways in which familiar chords are used in unfamiliar ways to expand the range of sounds available in a chord progressions: modal interchange and secondary dominants. In this chapter we will discuss how familiar chords may be altered as another way of finding new sounds within both diatonic and chromatic progressions.

Tension and Resolution

One of the basic forces in traditional harmonic progressions is the movement of *tension* toward *resolution,* that is, the movement of dissonance toward consonance. It is seen most frequently in the movement of the relatively dissonant dominant seventh chord toward the consonant tonic major or minor chord. This is true whether the movement is from the actual V7 of the key to the I or whether it is from a secondary dominant to its chord of (temporary) resolution. An unresolved chord has the power to make listeners uncomfortable or tense, and this tension ordinarily needs to be removed or resolved before a piece of music is considered to be properly finished. Of course, experienced composers and improvisors are well aware of how these feelings can be manipulated, and modern music is full of deliberately unresolved tension, testing the sophistication of the audience.

One way that tension may be increased in order to make the ultimate resolution more dramatic is by *altering notes of the dominant seventh chord*, i.e., raising or lowering them a half step. This means replacing some of the diatonic tones within the chord with chromatic tones, creating more dissonant intervals leading up to the consonant resolution. Other chord types—major and minor—may be altered as well (for example, mi(ma7), ma7(♯11), and even the augmented triad, which can be seen as a major triad with a raised fifth), but alterations are used most often on dominant chords because the effect of tension and resolution is most clearly expressed.

Building Altered Chords

The quality of the dominant seventh chord is essentially defined by the combination of the root, major third, and minor seventh degrees. If any of these notes are altered, the chord will take on a different name or quality. (The perfect fifth, while part of the basic chord structure, does not determine its quality; in other words, if the fifth is removed from a dominant seventh chord voicing, the chord quality is still identifiable.) This means that the tones that are available for alteration are the fifth, plus the ninth, eleventh, and thirteenth, previously seen as extensions and also called *color tones* because they add "color" to a chord without changing its essential quality.

Altered chord symbols are created by writing the symbol for chord quality (major, minor, or most often, dominant), followed by the note or notes that have been altered in parentheses, for example, C7(♭9). The exception is the raised (augmented) fifth, which is indicated by a plus sign before the seventh, as in D+7. (The augmented triad is symbolized by the plus sign added to the letter name of the chord, as in D+; although it is not a seventh chord, it usually functions as an altered V chord.) A chord may contain more than one alteration, in which case both alterations are indicated in parentheses and are written on top of each other, with the largest number above, as in G7(♭9♭5).

On the staff, altered chords are built by following the chord symbol and including all of the notes necessary to the basic chord structure as well as the indicated alterations. For now, voicings will be written with the notes in order, from lowest to highest. Also, keep in mind that flats and sharps in the chord symbol may not always mean the use of flats and sharps on the staff—flat means "lowered" and sharp means "raised," either of which may be accomplished in certain keys by the use of a natural sign.

EXERCISE 1

Build the altered chords on the staff including all of the notes indicated in the voicing from lowest to highest.

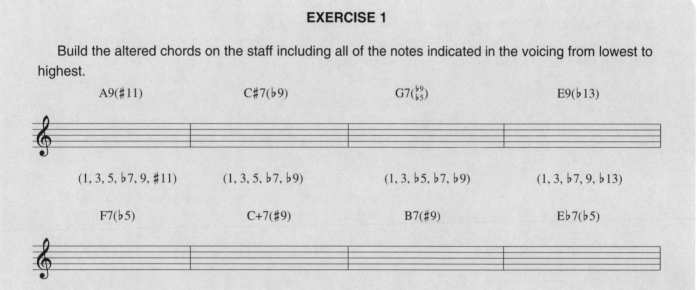

EXERCISE 2

Identify the altered chords, writing the chord symbol for each above the staff. In each voicing, the root is the lowest note.

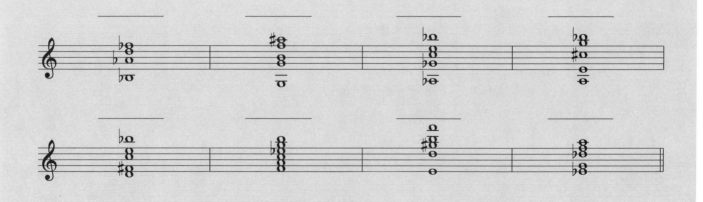

Chromatic Voice Leading

As discussed in Chapter 15, when chords are combined to form a progression, the way in which the notes of one chord connect to the notes of the next in the smoothest way is called *voice leading*. In the case of altered chords, the alterations are specifically chosen to create *chromatic voice leading*, that is, half-step connections from the notes of the dominant chord (and the altered tones in particular) to the notes of the chord of resolution. The chromatic tones may resolve by moving either down or up; as a general rule, *raised tones resolve upward* while *lowered tones resolve downward.*

The chord progressions in the following exercise illustrate common examples of voice leading resulting from the use of alterations on dominant chords.

EXERCISE 3

In each example, write the chord symbol above each chord on the staff. Accidentals apply throughout each bar.

Raised fifth (+): The raised fifth of the dominant chord resolves *upward* a half step to the major third of the chord of resolution:

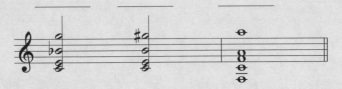

Lowered fifth (♭5): The lowered fifth of the dominant chord resolves *downward* a half step to the root of the chord of resolution:

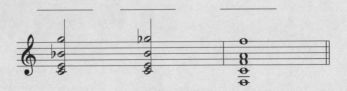

Raised ninth (♯9): The raised ninth of the dominant chord resolves *upward* a half step to the major seventh of the chord of resolution:

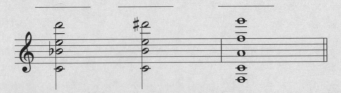

Lowered ninth (♭9): The lowered ninth of the dominant chord resolves *downward* a half step to the perfect fifth of the chord of resolution:

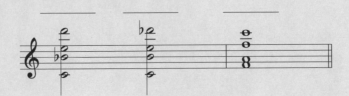

EXERCISE 3 (cont'd)

Raised eleventh (♯11): The raised eleventh of the dominant chord resolves *upward* a half step to the major ninth of the chord of resolution:

Lowered thirteenth (♭13): The lowered thirteenth of the dominant chord resolves *downward* a half step to the major ninth of the chord of resolution:

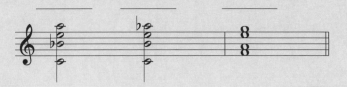

If more than one alteration is used in a chord, each alteration resolves up or down according to the rules for single alterations. For example, in the following progression, the raised fifth resolves upward and the lowered ninth resolves downward.

Fig. 1: voice leading with multiple alterations

EXERCISE 4

Write the chords on the staff using proper voice leading.

1.   C9   C7(♭9)   Fma7

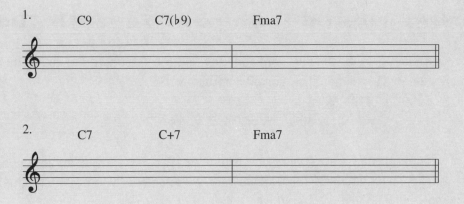

2.   C7   C+7   Fma7

Altered Scales

24

We have seen how major scales, minor scales, and their related diatonic harmonies are inseparable from one another; for each scale there are related chords, and for every chord there are related scales. The same idea holds true for nondiatonic chords and scales. In this chapter, we will look at how scales can be created to fit any type of altered chord, starting with the notes of the chords themselves. Scales that are related to altered chords are commonly called *altered scales,* and there are several that are commonly used.

EXERCISE 1

Analyze this progression, identifying the key and the function of each chord within the key.

F6/9	Dmi7	Gmi9	C7($^{\flat13}_{\flat9}$)

function: _____   _____   _____   _____   KEY: _____

What scale or scales will work as a source of melodies over this progression? Although all of the chords are diatonic in terms of their scale position and basic quality, the V chord contains alterations that, by definition, are outside the diatonic key center scale. What is the "right" scale to serve as a source of melodies over this particular chord? Composers and improvisers confront this question regularly and need a consistent, clearly understood method for arriving at a solution.

The basic method is this:

1. Write the altered chord on the staff.
2. Tip it over so that the notes are written horizontally within one octave.
3. Fill in the blanks.

Most altered chords are dominant chords, either functioning or nonfunctioning. (See the chapter on secondary dominants for a discussion of these terms.) Here are some altered dominant chords with their most practical scale solutions.

Functioning Altered Dominant Seventh Chords

This is a blanket name for a functioning dominant seventh (or extended dominant) chord with any alteration or combination of alterations. The possible alterations are:

$$\flat9 \quad \sharp9 \quad \flat5 \text{ or } \sharp11 \quad \sharp5 \text{ or } \flat13$$

The choice of whether to name an enharmonic alteration $\flat5$ or $\sharp11$, for example, depends on the direction of the resolution. If the alteration resolves upward, it should be named with a sharp, as in $\sharp11$ or $\sharp5$. If it resolves downward, it should be named with a flat, as in $\flat5$ or $\flat13$.

All of these alterations would not typically be voiced in a single chord, but it is possible to construct a scale that contains all of these notes. This "one size fits all" scale could then be used over *any* functioning altered dominant chord, that is, any altered V7 chord (including secondary dominants) that is resolving to its tonic.

Following the method for creating altered scales described above, the first step is to write a dominant chord on the staff including every possible alteration (including the harmonic equivalents).

Fig. 1: C altered dominant

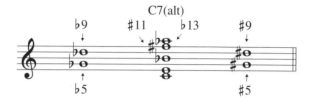

Now "tip the chord over," and write the notes of the chord horizontally on the staff within one octave, writing the harmonic function of each note beneath the staff, including enharmonic equivalents:

Fig. 2: C altered scale

This scale, commonly called the *altered scale,* contains all of the possible notes in the chord, so there are no "blanks" left to fill in. Although it actually contains only seven different tones, the same as a diatonic scale, the structure looks odd on the staff because the flat nine and sharp nine share the same letter name and the enharmonic equivalents are included. When this scale is played on an instrument, though, it will become clear that it has only seven distinct tones. As described previously, the choice of which particular enharmonic name is correct will depend on the context in which it is used.

EXERCISE 2

Write the following altered scales on the staff.

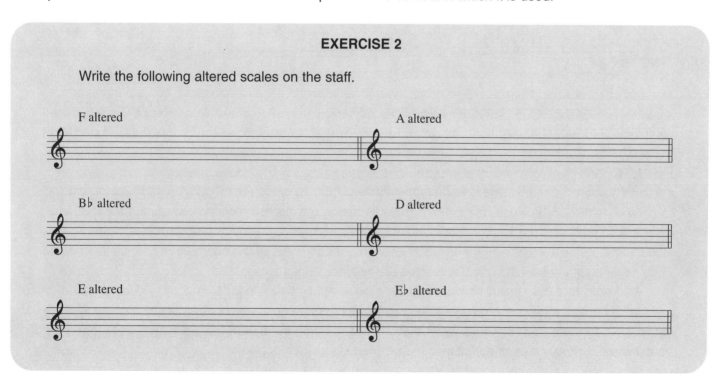

There are other scale solutions in common use that apply to specific functioning dominant chords. Two of these, the diminished scale and the whole tone scale, will be discussed in a later chapter. Other solutions involve the use of modes of the harmonic minor or melodic minor scales. In fact, the altered scale is often described as the seventh mode of melodic minor, e.g., "B altered is the seventh mode of C melodic minor." This way of thinking gives rise to formulas for improvising over altered chords such as, "Over an altered dominant chord, play melodic minor up a half step." These formulas can help a player react to unfamiliar sounds more quickly by narrowing attention to familiar patterns on an instrument, but they do not explain the relationships between melody and harmony as clearly as the direct comparison between the alterations and the chord structure illustrated by the altered scale.

Nonfunctioning Altered Dominant Seventh Chords

Since a nonfunctioning dominant chord by definition does not resolve to a tonic, most of the alterations that could possibly be used on a chord of this type simply sound awkwardly unresolved, and the altered scale has the same effect when used as a source of melodies. The only alteration that is commonly used in practice on a nonfunctioning dominant chord is the raised eleventh. To come up with the best scale solution for this chord, apply the same method as already described.

EXERCISE 3

Write C7(♯11) vertically on the staff, then write it horizontally, keeping all of the notes within one octave. Wherever there is a missing note, fill in the blank with the diatonic extension. Identify the harmonic function of each note.

C7(♯11)

function: _____ _____ _____ _____ _____ _____ _____ _____

The resulting scale is commonly called the *Lydian dominant* (or "Lydian flat seven") scale because it combines the raised fourth (as in the Lydian mode) with a lowered seventh (as found in the dominant seventh chord). The name essentially describes the structure, making a separate interval formula unnecessary.

The Lydian dominant scale is also commonly described as the fourth mode of melodic minor, e.g., "C Lydian dominant is the fourth mode of G melodic minor," giving rise to an improvisation formula, e.g., "Over a C7(♯11) chord, play G melodic minor." Again, while this is a quick way to find a pattern on an instrument, it doesn't describe the actual relationship of the notes to the chord, so it is of limited help in truly understanding how the chord and scale are related.

Also note that the Lydian dominant scale is often applied over *unaltered* nonfunctioning dominant seventh chords simply to create some melodic variety. Experienced players often take liberties with the strict, note-for-note rules of chord/scale relationships, treating them more as guidelines, but a good ear and sense of style are requirements.

EXERCISE 4

Write the following Lydian dominant scales on the staff.

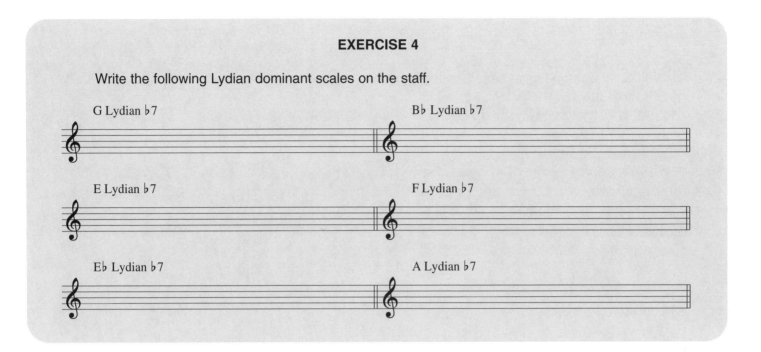

G Lydian ♭7   B♭ Lydian ♭7

E Lydian ♭7   F Lydian ♭7

E♭ Lydian ♭7   A Lydian ♭7

Summary of Altered Chord Scales

Analyzing altered chords and constructing scales to go with them may seem like a fairly complicated process, but in fact the two scales described above can be applied in most situations in which an altered scale is necessary. The basic rule for their application is as follows:

> For *functioning* dominant chords, use the *altered* scale.
> For *nonfunctioning* dominant chords, use the *Lydian dominant* scale.

There are other altered scales that will be described in later chapters, but these two scales cover the widest possible range of applications over altered dominant chords. In the everyday world of popular and standard jazz harmony, it is rare to come across altered chords other than the ones that have been discussed in this chapter.

When (nondominant) major or minor chords contain alterations, there is usually an existing scale (either a mode of the major scale or an altered minor scale) that matches the sound.

EXERCISE 5

What scales or modes already studied in this book provide melodic solutions for the following nondominant chord types?

chord	scale
ma7(♯11) or ma7(♭5)	_____
mi(ma7)	_____
mi7(♭5)	_____

EXERCISE 6

Analyze the chord progression. Locate key centers, and name an appropriate scale choice for each nondiatonic chord.

Gmi	Gmi(ma7)	Gmi7	Gmi6

function: _____   _____   _____   _____

scale: _____

Ebma7	Cmi7	Ami7(b5)	D7(b9,b13)

_____   _____   _____   _____

Gmi9	Cmi7 F+7(b9)	Bbma7	Cmi7 F+7(#9)

_____   _____   _____   _____

Bbma7	Ab7(#11)	Gmi7	Ami7(b5) D+7(b9)

_____   _____   _____   _____   _____

Diminished Seventh Chords

25

The diminished seventh chord has already appeared once, functioning as the VII°7 chord in the harmonic minor scale. In this chapter, we will look at diminished seventh chords outside this diatonic setting and see how their unique structure affects their role in chromatic harmony.

The structure of a diminished seventh chord has already been described as a diminished triad with an added diminished seventh interval above the root.

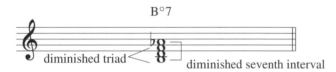

Looking carefully again at the structure of the diminished seventh chord, you might notice that it is made up entirely of minor third intervals stacked on top of each other. This structure produces an unexpected result: because all of the notes are an equal distance apart, any of the notes may function as the root, and therefore the diminished chord may have four different names.

EXERCISE 1

Build the four diminished chords named below, and compare the notes in each.

The Function of the Diminished Seventh Chord

The fact that the diminished chord has four possible roots means that its relationship to the chords around it is more complex than for other chords. Outside of the diatonic system, diminished chords can function in two main ways.

Function #1: As a substitution for the dominant seventh chord

---

EXERCISE 2

Name these chords in the key of C major.

chord name: _____   _____   _____   _____

These examples show two ways of resolving to a I chord. In the first example, a first inversion V7 (G7) chord resolves to I (C); in the second example, a root position VII°7 (B°7) chord also resolves to I. As you can see from the similar structure of the two chords, they achieve the same purpose from different directions: the root of the V7 chord resolves down a fifth, and the root of the VII°7 resolves up a half step. This means that a diminished seventh chord built on the leading tone (major seventh degree) of a major or minor scale may function as a *substitution* for the V7 chord in the same key; in other words, it may replace the existing V7 chord and create a different path to the same resolution. The relationship of the V7 and the VII°7 resolving to the same tonic chord was already seen within the harmonic minor scale harmony, so in a sense this is nothing new. However, the difference now is that this relationship is used *outside* of the diatonic structure, in major keys as well as minor.

Diminished chords are usually named according to which of the four notes is in the bass. The function is not affected by the chord name; therefore, any of the four diminished seventh chords may function as a substitution for a single dominant seventh chord.

Fig. 2: vii°7 chords resolving to I

Each of these diminished seventh chords contains the note B, which is the leading tone of the C major scale. As long as the leading tone is contained anywhere in the chord, it is functioning as a VII°7 chord.

Going one step further, the function of the diminished seventh chord as a substitution for the V7 chord can also be applied to secondary dominants.

EXERCISE 3

Analyze this progression.

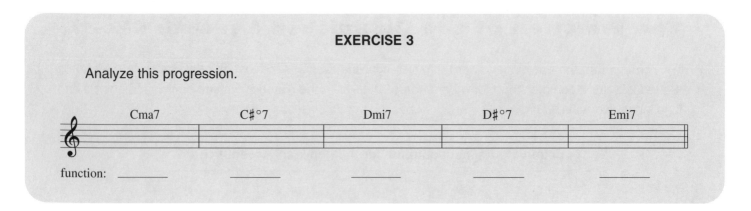

The C♯°7 chord is followed by Dmi7. Since C♯ is the leading tone of D, the C♯°7 is functioning as the VII°7 of D, substituting for A7, the V7 of D. Since Dmi7 is the IImi chord of the key center of C major, the function of C♯°7 is written as VII°7/II (spoken as "seven diminished of two"). Likewise, the D♯°7 contains the leading tone of Emi7, the IIImi chord of the key, so it is analyzed as VII°7/III.

Chapter 25

> ### Function #2: As a passing chord

A *passing chord* is a nondiatonic chord that connects the notes of two diatonic chords, in effect "passing" between the two.

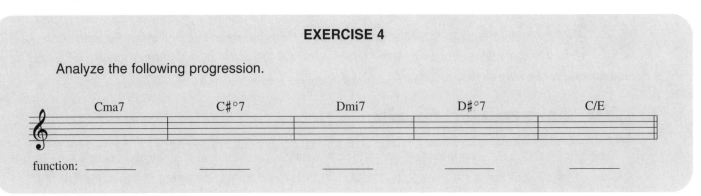

EXERCISE 4

Analyze the following progression.

| Cma7 | C#°7 | Dmi7 | D#°7 | C/E |

function: _____   _____   _____   _____   _____

The first diminished seventh chord, C#°7, contains the leading tone of the next chord, Dmi7, just as in the previous progression, so it is analyzed as VII°7/II. The second diminished chord, however, does not contain the leading tone of the following chord. The C triad with E in the bass is a first inversion I triad, and its leading tone is B, which is *not* one of the four tones in the D#°7 chord. Therefore, this diminished chord cannot be analyzed as a substitution for a secondary dominant. The alternative is to call it a passing chord, connecting the notes of Dmi7 to the notes of C/E. The function of a passing chord is indicated simply by its number and quality, so D#°7 is analyzed as #II°7 ("sharp two diminished seventh").

Summary of the rules for analyzing the function of diminished seventh chords

1. If *any* of the four notes of the diminished seventh chord is the leading tone of the following chord, it is functioning as a *vii°* chord, or dominant substitute.
2. If *none* of the notes of the diminished seventh chord are the leading tone of the following chord, it is functioning as a *passing chord*.

EXERCISE 5

Analyze the following progression.

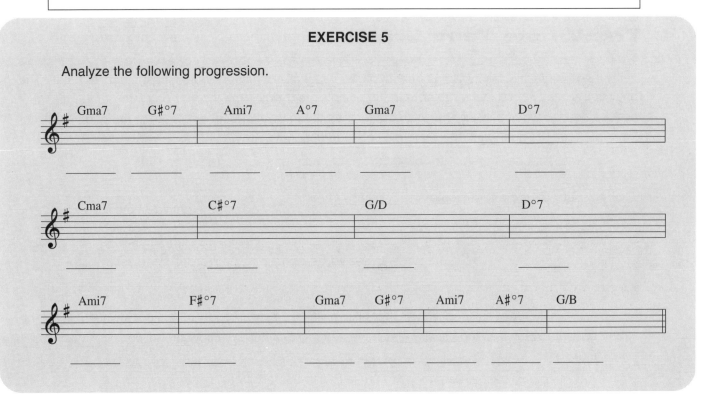

26 Symmetrical Scales

A *symmetrical scale* is a scale that is built from a repetitive pattern of intervals. There are three symmetrical scales in common use: the *chromatic scale*, the *whole tone scale*, and the *diminished scale*. In this chapter, we will look at the structure of each scale and its relationship to the surrounding harmony.

The Chromatic Scale

The chromatic scale is composed entirely of half steps, resulting in a total of twelve tones to the octave. Depending on whether the scale is ascending or descending, the tones of the scale are notated with either sharps or flats, as shown here.

Fig. 1: the C chromatic scale

Because of its structure, the chromatic scale is not tonal in the same way that a diatonic scale is tonal; that is, there is no single note around which the other notes of the scale revolve. Since all of the notes are an equal distance apart, any note could serve as a tonic. Given this lack of tonality, the chromatic scale as such is not used as a source of melodies or harmonies in popular music in the same way diatonic scales are. (The chromatic scale does have this role in music that is deliberately nontonal, or "atonal.") Individual chromatic tones show up in a diatonic context as parts of altered chords, chromatic chord progressions, and as passing tones between diatonic scale tones. Thus, the chromatic scale as a complete structure exists more in theory than in practice and is mainly useful for illustrating the proper notation of chromatic tones.

The Whole Tone Scale

This symmetrical scale gets its name because it is built entirely of whole steps, or whole tones. The result is a scale with six steps rather than the usual seven, which means that one letter of the alphabet must be omitted when building the scale. As long as the interval structure is correct, the gap may occur anywhere, and the spelling of the scale may change depending on its direction.

Fig. 2: the C whole tone scale

Because this scale, like the chromatic scale, is composed of a single interval pattern all the way through, any scale tone could function as the tonic, giving it a similar tonal ambiguity. However, unlike the chromatic scale, the whole tone scale does have a practical function in popular music.

An analysis of the whole tone scale shows that it contains the root, third, and seventh of a dominant seventh chord, plus both alterations of the fifth. (The ninth is unaltered.) Some scale tones are spelled differently depending on whether they are ascending or descending.

Fig. 3: analysis of the whole tone scale

| function: | 1 | 9 | 3 | #11 | #5 | b7 | (8) | (8) | b7 | b13 | b5 | 3 | 9 | 1 |

Note that the b5 and #11 are enharmonic, as are the #5 and b13. This means that, in simplified terms, *the whole tone scale may be used as a chord scale for any functioning dominant ninth chord with an altered fifth (e.g., C+9).*

EXERCISE 1

Write the following whole tone scales on the staff.

C# whole tone

E whole tone

A whole tone

Bb whole tone

G whole tone

Eb whole tone

The Diminished Scale

The diminished scale is a symmetrical scale built from alternating whole steps and half steps, resulting in a scale with eight different tones. The "extra" note requires that one letter name be duplicated. There is no precise formula for where this duplication should occur; as long as the order of whole steps and half steps is correct, any spelling is acceptable.

Fig. 4: the C diminished scale

EXERCISE 2

Build the following diminished scales on the staff. Begin each scale with a whole step, followed by a half step, then a whole step, etc. as shown above.

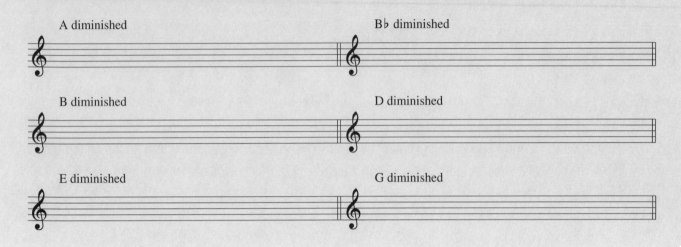

The diminished scale can serve at least two possible functions:

1. As a scale for a diminished chord

The diminished scale functions as the chord scale for any diminished seventh chord, regardless of whether the chord is functioning as a VII° chord or a passing chord. The scale is built from the root of the chord, beginning with a whole step.

EXERCISE 3

Write a G diminished seventh chord on the staff, followed by a G diminished scale.

Notice that the G diminished scale contains all four notes of the G diminished seventh chord, with the scale following a pattern of a whole step then a half step above each chord tone. For this reason, when the diminished scale is used as the chord scale of a diminished seventh chord, it is often called the *whole-half diminished scale.*

2. As a scale for an altered dominant chord

We have seen how the VII°7 chord may substitute for a functioning dominant seventh chord to create a different-sounding resolution, for example when B°7 is used in place of G7 to resolve to C. Based on the same idea, the *scale* of the VII°7 chord may be used over the V7 chord itself to create alterations in the melody; that is, the harmony (G7) stays the same but the substitute *melody* (the B diminished scale) is used in place of the normal diatonic scale.

EXERCISE 4

Write the one-octave B diminished scale on the staff.

Now write the B diminished scale again, this time with G as the lowest tone. Below the staff, write the function of each scale tone in relation to G.

function: _____

Notice that when the B diminished scale is rearranged so that G is the lowest tone, the order of whole steps and half steps in relation to the starting note is reversed; that is, from G, the first interval is a half step, followed by a whole step, and so on. This application of the diminished scale, as an altered dominant chord scale, is commonly known as the *half-whole diminished scale*, or the *dominant diminished scale*. From the root of the dominant chord, the half-step/whole-step pattern results in a dominant scale with these alterations:

♭9   ♯9   ♯11/♭5

In common practice, the dominant diminished scale is used as a chord scale for *any functioning dominant chord with an altered ninth*. As a rule, if the chord contains an altered fifth, the altered or whole tone scales are used.

EXERCISE 5

Write the dominant diminished scale from each of the following roots.

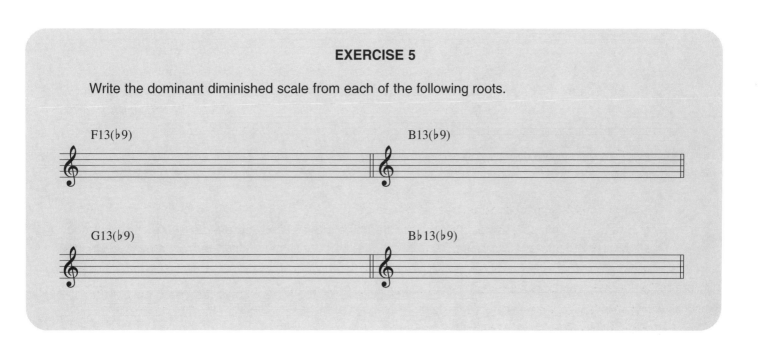

Symmetrical Scale Summary

The function of each symmetrical scale can be summarized as follows:

Scale	Function
Chromatic	proper notation of chromatic tones
Whole Tone	chord scale for functioning dominant ninth chords with *altered fifths*
Diminished	*Whole-half:* chord scale for diminished seventh chord. *Half-whole (dominant diminished* scale): chord scale for functioning dominant chords with *altered ninths and natural fifths*

NOTE: The altered scale contains elements of both the the dominant diminished and whole tone scales and is therefore sometimes referred to as the diminished/whole tone scale. *Review its construction, and compare it to both symmetrical scales to see why this is so.*

EXERCISE 6

Analyze the following chord progression, and identify the scale possibilities, including key center scales and symmetrical scales.

EXERCISE 7

Identify the scales used in the following melody by analyzing their relationship to the chords around them.

scale: _____   _____

_____   _____   _____

Diatonic Chord Substitution

27

The diatonic system is extremely effective for organizing melodies and harmonies into pleasing patterns in a great many styles of music. As in any system that is used over a long period of time, however, people have a need to create change. Certain composers and improvisers in classical music and jazz (at least in those styles generally categorized as "art" music, as opposed to "popular" music) have at various times reacted against the simplicity and over-familiarity of the diatonic system by going the opposite way, into atonality. Popular music, which is familiar by definition, is unlikely to evolve too far in that direction. Instead, popular musicians look for variety within the diatonic system by combining the familiar elements in new ways. We have looked at several of these ways: chord inversion, extension, and alteration; modal interchange; and secondary dominants. Another way is by *chord substitution*. This means replacing the obvious, expected chord with another that is slightly different but that still accomplishes the same function. When the substitute chord belongs to the same harmonized scale as the original chord, the method is called *diatonic substitution*.

The way that substitutions are chosen is by grouping the diatonic chords into families of related sounds and exchanging one for another. This does not mean that the chords are completely interchangable, but rather that there are options within each family to create different voice leading and subtle emotional variations. The exchange of related chords to create different-sounding progressions while staying within the original structure is called *reharmonization*.

Chord Families

Chords in the major or minor diatonic system may be seen as belonging to one of three main families, each with a basic harmonic tendency or effect:

1. The family of the I chord is called the *tonic* family. Its basic effect is to temporarily or permanently resolve a piece of music. It is a place of rest, or "home."
2. The family of the IV chord is called the *subdominant* family. Its basic effect is to move away from the I chord.
3. The family of the V chord is called the *dominant* family. Its basic effect is to move toward (resolve to) the I chord.

The basic effect of each of these families can be most easily seen in a blues progression consisting only of the main chords I, IV, and V.

EXERCISE 1

Below each chord of this blues in C, write the chord's scale step number (I, IV, or V), family name (tonic, subdominant, or dominant), and effect ("home," "away," or "toward").

scale step: _____   _____ _____ _____ _____

family name: _____   _____ _____ _____ _____

effect: _____   _____ _____ _____ _____

The remaining diatonic chords—IImi, IIImi, VImi, and VII°—each belong to one of the three families. These families are slightly different in major and minor keys.

Major Key Diatonic Substitution

The major key diatonic chord families are as follows:

Tonic family:	I, IIImi, and VImi
Subdominant family:	IV and IImi
Dominant family:	V and VII°

The "family relationship" may be seen by comparing the structures of the chords in each family to each other.

EXERCISE 2

On the staff, write the triads of each major-key family in root position in C major. Notice how many notes the chords within each family have in common. (The same relationships exist for seventh chords, but the structures may be more easily compared with triads.)

Tonic   Subdominant   Dominant

Using diatonic substitution, the blues progression can be transformed into something with a much different sound, yet with the same overall chord movement.

EXERCISE 3

Below each chord, write its scale step number, and below that, its chord family.

C   Ami   Emi   %.   F   Dmi

scale step: _____

chord family: _____

C   Ami   G   B°   C   %.

_____

_____

Minor Key Diatonic Substitution

In minor keys, the chord families are slightly different due to the different scale structure and, therefore, different relationship between chord roots:

Tonic family:	Imi and ♭III
Subdominant family:	IVmi, II°, and ♭VI
Dominant family:	Vmi and ♭VII (or V and VII°*)

NOTE: As discussed in previous chapters, it is very common in minor keys to replace the v minor chord in the diatonic natural minor harmonized scale with the V or V7 chord, while at the same time the ♭VII chord is replaced with the vii° chord. Although the sounds are different, the same family relationships exist either way.

EXERCISE 4

On the staff, write the triads of each minor-key family in root position (in A minor). Again, notice how many notes the chords in each family have in common.

Tonic   Subdominant   Dominant

The blues progression (in this case a minor blues) may be used again to illustrate the application of diatonic substitution in minor keys.

EXERCISE 5

Below each chord of this blues in A minor, write its scale step number (Imi, IVmi, or Vmi), family name (tonic, subdominant, or dominant), and effect ("home," "away," or "toward").

Ami   ⁒   ⁒   ⁒   Dmi   ⁒   Ami   ⁒   Emi   ⁒   Ami   ⁒

scale step: _____   _____   _____   _____   _____

family name: _____   _____   _____   _____   _____

effect: _____   _____   _____   _____   _____

Again, using diatonic substitution, the progression could be transformed into something much different-sounding, but with the same overall effect in the chord motion.

EXERCISE 6

Below each chord, write its scale step number and below that, its chord family.

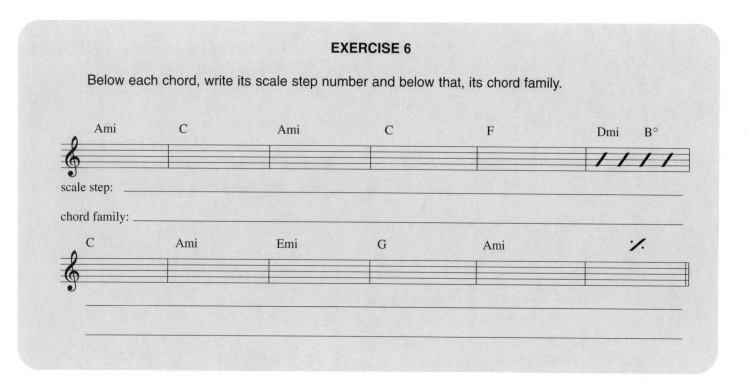

scale step: _____

chord family: _____

NOTE: In triad-based styles of music, the vii° chord in major and the ii° chord in minor, being diminished triads, stand out from the other major and minor triads due to their dissonance. In order to suggest those substitutions but avoid odd-sounding harmonies, it is very common to use the first inversion V triad in place of the vii° triad in major keys, and the first inversion ♭VII triad in place of the ii° triad in minor keys. Replace the diminished triads in Exercises 3 and 6 with these chords to hear the difference. Chord inversion and chord substitution are two ways of achieving the same goal of increasing variety within the diatonic structure, and they are closely related to each other.

Melodic Substitution

Diatonic substitution is used not only as a system of chord-for-chord replacement of harmonies. It is also seen in cases where the original harmony is retained and a *melody* based on the substitute chord is played over it. This is a very common way for improvisors to increase the amount of melodic variety over typical harmonies.

For example, compare the notes of an E minor seventh arpeggio to the notes of a C major seventh chord:

Fig. 1: melodic substitution

The Emi7 arpeggio contains the notes E, G, B, and D, which are the major third, perfect fifth, major seventh, and major ninth degrees of C. Thus, an E minor seventh arpeggio used as a source of melodies over a C major seventh chord will produce the effect of C major ninth.

In the same way, explore the relationship of each diatonic substitution to its parent chord to find the added melodic color that results.

EXERCISE 7

In each case, write the arpeggio of the diatonic substitution on the staff, and compare its tones to those of the parent chord to see the melodic relationship.

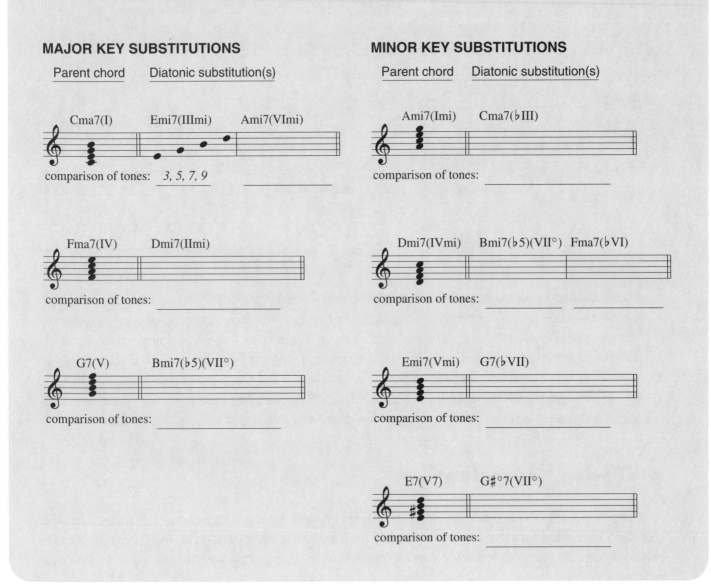

MAJOR KEY SUBSTITUTIONS

Parent chord | Diatonic substitution(s)

Cma7(I) | Emi7(IIImi) | Ami7(VImi)

comparison of tones: *3, 5, 7, 9*

Fma7(IV) | Dmi7(IImi)

comparison of tones:

G7(V) | Bmi7(♭5)(VII°)

comparison of tones:

MINOR KEY SUBSTITUTIONS

Parent chord | Diatonic substitution(s)

Ami7(Imi) | Cma7(♭III)

comparison of tones:

Dmi7(IVmi) | Bmi7(♭5)(VII°) | Fma7(♭VI)

comparison of tones:

Emi7(Vmi) | G7(♭VII)

comparison of tones:

E7(V7) | G♯°7(VII°)

comparison of tones:

Diatonic chord substitution and melodic substitution are tools that are used every day by writers, arrangers, and improvisors alike. While the principles are fairly simple, they are not infallible formulas—becoming a skilled user of these ideas takes practice and a critical ear. As in everything musical, taste and style are essential elements that no theory can provide.

Flat Five Substitution

28

Another type of chord substitution that is used in popular music, especially jazz-influenced styles, is commonly called *flat five substitution*. This occurs when a functioning dominant seventh chord is replaced by the dominant seventh chord with its root a flat (diminished) fifth interval away. As in diatonic substitution, the result is a change in the bass line and voice leading *without* a change in the overall chord function. Flat five substitution is possible because the two dominant seventh chords share the same *tritone* interval.

The Tritone

"Tritone" is another name for an augmented fourth/diminished fifth interval, which can also be described as an interval made up of three whole steps, hence the name "*tri*-tone."

Fig. 1: the tritone

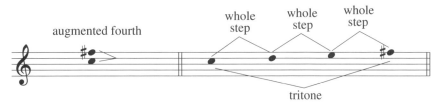

All dominant seventh chords contain a tritone interval between the major third degree and the minor seventh degree.

Fig. 2: the tritone in dominant seventh chords

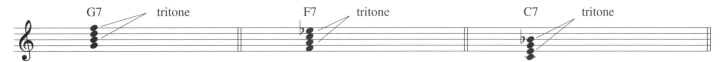

The tritone is a dissonant interval, and this dissonance at the heart of the dominant seventh chord is what gives the chord the feeling of "wanting" to resolve to the consonant major or minor tonic chord. In flat five substitution, the substitute chord contains the same tritone as the original dominant seventh chord, meaning that it can resolve to the same tonic even though it is built on an entirely different root. (Due to the tritone relationship, flat five substitution is also called *tritone substitution*.)

EXERCISE 1

Write these dominant seventh chords on the staff in root position.

What is the third of G7? _____   What is the seventh of D♭7? _____

What is the seventh of G7? _____   What is the third of D♭7? _____

Although the roles of the notes are reversed, the thirds and sevenths of the two chords form the same tritone interval (B and C♭ are enharmonic) and thus have the same harmonic effect.

Fig. 3: resolution of the tritone to the tonic chord

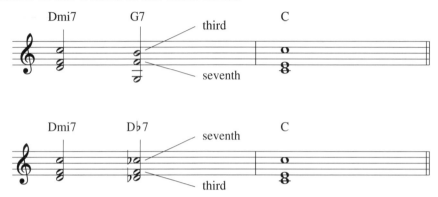

In the above example, the third degree of G7, B, resolves *up* a half step to the root of the tonic chord, C, while the seventh degree of G7, F, resolves *down* a half step to the third degree of the C major triad, E. On the D♭7 chord, the third degree, F, resolves *down* a half step to the third degree of C, while the seventh degree of D♭7, C♭ (enharmonic with B), resolves *up* a half step to C.

Analysis of Flat Five Substitution

The most obvious result of flat five substitution is a chromatic descending bass line rather than a bass line moving in fourths and fifths. As seen above, the bass line descends in half steps from Dmi7 to D♭7 to C, rather than jumping from Dmi7 to G7 to C. This creates smoother voice leading in the bass without changing the harmonic tendency of the chords.

The substitute chord is analyzed as "♭II7" ("flat two seven"). In addition to our normal V7–I relationship, we can now add the fact that a dominant seventh chord may resolve down a half step (♭II7–I). It must be stressed that this only works with *functioning* dominant seventh chords. A dominant seventh chord that does not resolve to its intended tonic may not be replaced in this way. Also, this substitution idea only applies to dominant seventh-type chords (including extensions and alterations), not to other chord types.

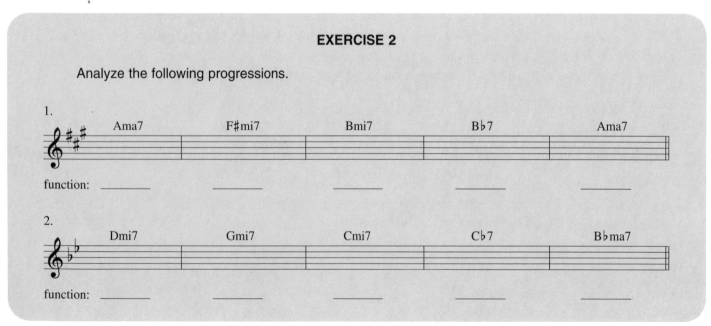

Chapter 28

Secondary Dominant Application

Flat five substitution may also be applied to functioning secondary dominants, as well as V7 chords in minor keys. In other words, it can apply to any dominant seventh chord that is resolving, even temporarily, to its tonic. The clue for the presence of flat five substitution is the descending chromatic bass line.

Like secondary dominants, flat five substitutions are analyzed according to their function. In the key of C major, for example, the progression G♭7–Fma7 is analyzed as "♭II7/IV–IVma7" ("flat two seven of four to four major seven").

EXERCISE 3

Analyze the following chord progressions.

1. Emi7 A7 Dmi7 G7 Cma7

function: ___ ___ ___ ___ ___

2. Emi7 E♭7 Dmi7 D♭7 Cma7

function: ___ ___ ___ ___ ___

3. Cmi C7 Fmi Dmi7(♭5) G7 Cmi

function: ___ ___ ___ ___ ___ ___

4. Cmi G♭7 Fmi Dmi7(♭5) D♭7 Cmi

function: ___ ___ ___ ___ ___ ___

Summary of Rules for Flat Five Substitution

1. Flat five substitution applies to functioning dominant seventh-type chords only, not to nonfunctioning dominant seventh chords or to other chord types.
2. Flat five substitution results in a chromatic descending bassline.
3. Flat five substitutions are analyzed according to their relationship to the chord of resolution, either the tonic of the key (♭II7–I) or the temporary resolution of a secondary dominant (e.g. ♭II7/IV).

To the ear, flat five substitution is a subtle change in the direction of the bassline, not a dramatic change in harmony. This means that, for example, a bass player can play a descending chromatic bassline while the guitarist plays the original IImi–V7–I progression, or vice versa. On-the-spot reharmonization is a basic element of jazz performance, and, with experience, musicians learn to judge how and when to use it.

Modulation

29

From our study of major and minor key centers, we have observed that a piece of music may start in one key and then go to one or more other keys before returning to the original. This change to a different key is called *modulation.* As with chromatic alterations and the various forms of substitution, the reason for modulation is mainly to achieve greater harmonic variety. There are two basic ways of modulating, called *direct* modulation and *pivot chord* modulation.

Direct Modulation

As the name implies, direct modulation is a change of key without any preparation. The effect is dramatic and decisive.

When analyzing a chord progression that includes direct modulation, indicate the original key at the beginning of the piece as shown below. It is understood that all chords following that indication are numbered in relation to that key. When the modulation occurs, indicate the new key directly below the first chord that belongs to it, with the understanding that all of the following chords are numbered in relation to that new key, rather than the original.

Fig. 1: analyzing direct modulation

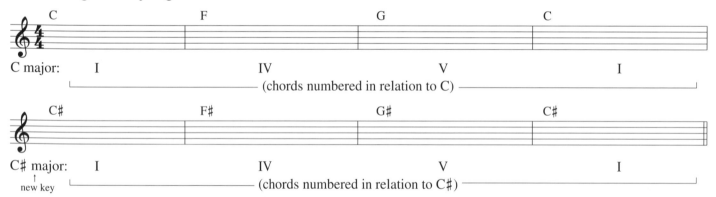

EXERCISE 1

Analyze the progressions below, and find the points at which direct modulation occurs.

In each case in Exercise 1, the key change is abrupt, with no hint in the preceding harmony that a change is about to occur. The second example, in which the key modulates up a half step, is a cliché in pop music arrangements, especially show tunes, when a sudden burst of energy is desired. Direct modulation best retains its dramatic effect when used sparingly.

Pivot Chord Modulation

This method of modulation uses a chord that is common to two keys as a way of leaving the old key and entering the new key. The chord that the two keys have in common is called the *pivot chord,* because from it the progression can "pivot" in either direction. The effect of pivot chord modulation is smooth and subtle, with the actual change of key sometimes going unnoticed until after it has occurred.

There are four steps in pivot chord modulation:

> **Step 1: Establishment of the original key**; creating a strong sense of tonality through the use of the primary chords (I, IV, and V).

> **Step 2: Use of a pivot chord**; the pivot chord belongs to both the original key and the new key. The best pivot chord is usually a chord with subdominant function (IV or IImi in major; IVmi, II°, or ♭VI in minor) that leads strongly to the V chord of the new key.

> **Step 3: Entry into the new key**; the new key is not established until a chord is used that belongs to the new key but not the old, usually the new V chord.

> **Step 4: Resolution in the new key**; resolving to the tonic of the new key securely establishes the new tonality.

In some progressions we have seen, which include secondary dominants or modal interchange, the feeling of a new tonic chord is hinted at but is followed by chords of the original key. In this case, no modulation has taken place as the new tonality has not been clearly established. A *real* modulation requires a series of chords that establish the new key without question. An important factor is time—if a new tonality lasts long enough, even without repeated resolutions to reinforce it, it will take hold in the listener's ear as a tonal center of its own.

Not all modulations are permanent. It is quite common to change to a new key to mark a significant new section of a song, such as a bridge, and then return to the original key. If the modulations are artfully managed, a great amount of harmonic variety can be achieved without ever losing the sense of structure that is central to popular harmony.

Analyzing Pivot Chord Modulation

Any analysis of a chord progression including a modulation must make it clear exactly where the new key begins so that, from that point on, the functions of the chords are numbered in relation to the new tonic. Establish the original key as before, and when the pivot chord occurs, write its function in both the old and new keys as shown in Figure 2.

Fig. 2: analyzing pivot chord modulation

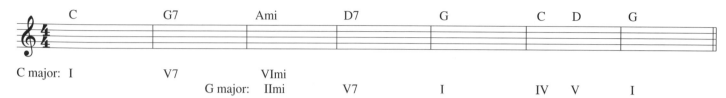

C	G7	Ami	D7	G	C D	G

C major: I V7 VImi
G major: IImi V7 I IV V I

EXERCISE 2

Analyze the following progressions. Find the pivot chords, and notate the analysis as described above.

1.

C	G7	C	F	Dmi	G7

Emi	A7	D	G	D	A7	D

2.

C Ami	F G7	C	Ami B7

Emi	F♯mi7(♭5) B7	Emi	./.

EXERCISE 3

Analyze each of the progressions below. Find out where the modulations occur and whether they are direct or pivot chord modulations.

1.

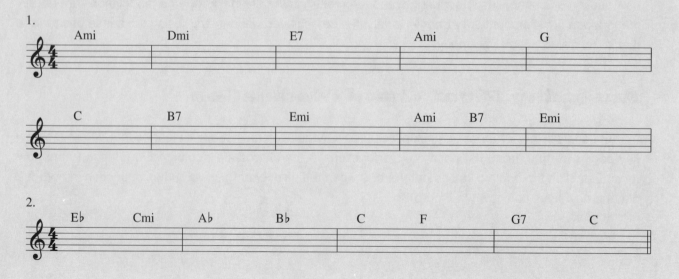

Ami	Dmi	E7	Ami	G

C	B7	Emi	Ami B7	Emi

2.

E♭ Cmi	A♭ B♭	C F	G7	C

Afterword

Assuming that you have now completed the final chapter of this book, take a moment to look back at the chart opposite the Introduction. What may at first glance have looked like a jumble of letters, numbers, dots, and symbols now reveals itself to be a whole series of patterns: a key; a rhythmic feel; a set of related chords with clearly notated qualities, extensions, and alterations; a melody derived from a scale and containing particular intervals; and so on. Before you even pick up an instrument to play this tune, you see before you everything you need to know in order to play the chords and melody and even plan a solo that fits the changes. Depending on your experience as a player and how well your fingers and ears cooperate with your brain, it may take seconds or perhaps hours to make it all sound musical, but the point is that you now have enough knowledge to do it in the first place. The information covered in this book more than covers the vast majority of day-to-day musical experiences that popular musicians encounter. While more complex theories are useful in understanding more complex styles of music, their application to popular styles becomes increasingly rare, while the simpler structures studied here are practically universal. It may take a bit more time and experience before you can glance at a tune and be able to interpret and play it on sight, but at this point there should no longer be any mystery as to how it's done.

As music evolves, and it always will, players will continue to create novel combinations of these building blocks. New sounds will become popular and require new names. What today seems strange and esoteric will tomorrow be considered ordinary. With the understanding you have gained of the basic structure of music, though, you will be able to absorb whatever comes around and quickly add it to your own vocabulary of ideas and sounds. We trust also that in learning this new language you find that you have given up none of the inspiration that drew you to music in the first place, but have only found a way to express it more easily and clearly to the rest of us, adding your voice to the worldwide musical conversation.

Appendix I: Chord Symbols

Chord symbols are the way that songwriters, arrangers, and players communicate written harmony to one another in the practical world of popular music. Any system of symbols is subject to interpretation by different people in different locations with different backgrounds, and chord symbols are no exception. Certain chord symbols are internationally understood, while others are local and quite prone to misinterpretation. Because of the constantly evolving nature of popular music and the fact that many if not most of the musicians performing it are not formally educated, it is unlikely that any one set of chord symbols will become and remain the acknowledged standard. The best approach is to be flexible, developing a consistent set of rules for naming chords that avoids vagueness and redundancy, while at the same time understanding the ambiguities of many traditional or regional names. Much of the communication between musicians, after all, depends much more upon the ear than the eye, so sometimes just playing the chord and reacting to the sound itself is more efficient and meaningful than debating the interpretation of a written symbol.

General Rules for Naming Chords

Taking into account the many ways in which chords may be symbolized, here are some general rules and recommendations worth noting.

- When no symbol follows the chord letter, a major triad is assumed—e.g., the symbol C by itself stands for a C major triad.
- The numbers 7, 9, or 13 alone next to the chord letter means that the chord is a dominant-quality chord—e.g., C9 is "C *dominant* ninth."
- The symbol "ma," meaning "major," is never used with a chord letter alone, as in "Cma." It is always used together with 7, 9, or 13, as in Cma7, Cma9, or Cma13, and means that the chord includes a major seventh.
- The symbol for a minor triad is the letter name of the chord plus "mi," as in "Cmi." The same symbol is used together with numbers to indicate other minor-quality chords such as Cmi7, Cmi6/9, Cmi11, etc.
- If the seventh is present in a chord, added tones are numbered as extensions. For example, adding a sixth to a C7 chord results in "C13." If the seventh is not present, the added tone is numbered as a simple interval, e.g., "C6."
- Chords with extensions are symbolized by the highest extension present in the chord. For example, C13 indicates a dominant seventh chord quality with an added thirteenth. (The other extensions may or may not actually be voiced in the chord, depending on other factors.)
- The symbol "+" refers to the augmented fifth only, not an augmented ninth or eleventh. For example, the symbol C+9 means "C dominant 9 augmented fifth," *not* "C augmented ninth."
- All alterations are written in parentheses, such as Cmi7($\flat$5). When more than one alteration is present, they are shown one above the other, with the largest alteration on top, such as C7($\substack{\flat 9 \\ \flat 5}$).
- $\sharp$11 chords may contain a natural fifth degree, but $\flat$5 chords do not.
- Eleventh chords may contain a third, but sus chords do not.

The following is a reference list of chord symbols based on the principles listed above. Also included are some common names that you should learn to recognize but that should generally be avoided due to their ambiguity. While it may never be possible to achieve total consistency in the world of chord symbols, a common-sense regard for clarity will go a long way.

TRIADS

SYMBOL	NAME	AVOID
C	C major	Cma, Cmaj
Cmi	C minor	C-, Cmin, Cm
C+	C augmented	C($\sharp$5), Caug, C+5
C°	C diminished	Cdim, C°(no7)
Csus	C suspended fourth	C(addF), C($\sharp$3)

TRIADS WITH ADDED NOTES

SYMBOL	NAME	AVOID
C6	C major sixth	Cmaj6th, C(addA)
Cmi6	C minor sixth	C-6, Cm+6
C6/9	C major six-nine	C6(add9), C13(no7)
Cmi6/9	C minor six-nine	C-6(+9), Cm13(omit7)
C2	C major add two	Cma(add2), C9(no7)
Cmi2	C minor add two	C-(+9), Cm9(omit7)

SEVENTH CHORDS

SYMBOL	NAME	AVOID
Cma7	C major seventh	C7, C$\triangle$, C7+, CM7
Cmi7	C minor seventh	C-7, Cm7, Cmin7
C7	C dominant seventh	C7, C(+7), C($\flat$7)
C+7	C dominant seventh augmented fifth	Caug7, C7($\sharp$5)
C°7	C diminished seventh	Cdim7, Cm6($\flat$5)
Cmi7($\flat$5)	C minor seventh (flat five)	C$^{\varnothing}$, C-7(-5), C°
Cmi(ma7)	C minor (major seventh)	Cmin°, C-7
C7sus	C seventh suspended fourth	C7 4

EXTENDED CHORDS

SYMBOL	NAME	AVOID
Cma9	C major ninth	C$\triangle$9, C7(+9)
Cmi9	C minor ninth	C-9, Cm7(9)
C9	C dominant ninth	C7(+9), C$_7^9$
C+9	C dominant ninth augmented fifth	Caug9, C9(+5)
Cmi9($\flat$5)	C minor ninth (flat five)	C$^{\varnothing}$9, C-9(+5)
C9sus	C ninth suspended fourth	C11, C9($\natural$11)
Cmi11	C minor eleventh	C-11, Cm7($^{11}_9$)
Cmi11($\flat$5)	C minor eleventh (flat five)	Cmin11(-5), C$^{\varnothing}$11
Cma13	C major thirteenth	C6(+7), C$\triangle$13
C13	C dominant thirteenth	C7(+A), C9($^{13}_{11}$)
C13sus	C thirteenth suspended fourth	C9($^{13}_4$), C13(11)

ALTERED CHORDS

SYMBOL	NAME	AVOID
Cma9($\flat$5)	C major ninth (flat five)	C$\triangle$9(-5), C$\triangle$($^{\sharp9}_{\sharp5}$)
Cma13($\sharp$11)	C major thirteenth (sharp eleven)	C$\triangle$($^{13}_{\sharp11}{}_9$)
C7($\flat$9)	C dominant seventh (flat nine)	C7-9, C$\flat$9
C9($^{\flat13}_{\sharp11}$)	C dominant ninth (flat 13, sharp 11)	C7($^{\sharp11}_{\flat13}$)
C13($^{\sharp11}_{\flat9}$)	C dominant thirteenth (sharp 11, flat nine)	C7($^{\flat9}_{\sharp11}{}_{\flat13}$)
C+7($\sharp$9)	C augmented seventh (sharp nine)	C7($^{\sharp9}_{\sharp5}$)

OTHER CHORDS

SYMBOL	NAME	AVOID
C5	C power chord	C(no 3)
C/D	C5 add two	Csus2, Cadd2
C/D	slash C over D (C triad with D in bass)	$\frac{C}{D}$ (pure)
$\frac{C}{D}$	polychord C over D (C triad over D triad)	C triad/D triad

Appendix II: Solutions to Exercises

Chapter 1

Ex. 3   (treble clef, l to r) C, G, A, D, F, F, D, E, B, G, E, C, D;

(bass clef, l to r) E, B, C, F, A, A, F, G, D, B, G, E, F

Ex. 4

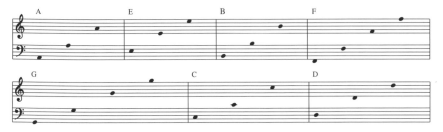

Ex. 5   (treble clef) C, D, F, A, B, E, E, B, A, C, G;

(bass clef) E, F, B, C, D, G, C, E, D

Ex. 6

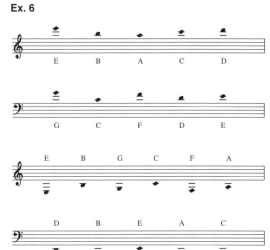

Chapter 2

Ex. 3   **Ex. 4**

Ex. 5   D major — 2 sharps (F♯, C♯); A major — 3 sharps (F♯, C♯, G♯); E major — 4 sharps (F♯, C♯, G♯, D♯); B major — 5 sharps (F♯, C♯, G♯, D♯, A♯)

F♯ major — 6 sharps (F♯, C♯, G♯, D♯, A♯, E♯); C♯ major — 7 sharps (F♯, C♯, G♯, D♯, A♯, E♯, B♯)

Ex. 6   (treble clef) A major; F♯ major, G major, E major; (bass clef) D major, B major, A major, C♯ major

Appendix II: Solutions to Exercises

Chapter 3

Ex. 3 **Ex. 4**

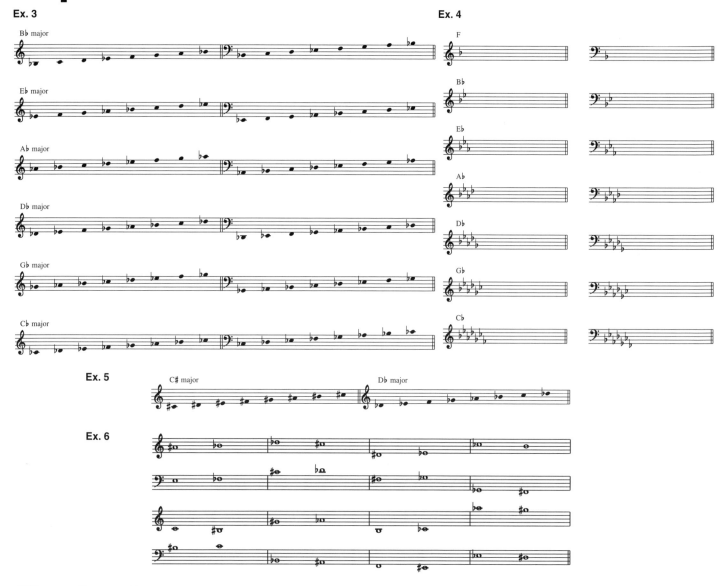

Ex. 5

Ex. 6

Chapter 4

Ex. 1 (treble) fourth, second, sixth; (bass) seventh, third, octave, fifth; (treble) second, octave, sixth, fourth; (bass) seventh, fifth, unison, third

Ex. 2 (treble) perfect 4th, major 2nd, major 6th; (bass) minor 7th, major 3rd, minor 7th, diminished 5th; (treble) augmented 4th, major 6th, minor 2nd, major 3rd; (bass) augmented 5th, major 7th, perfect 5th, perfect unison

Ex. 3

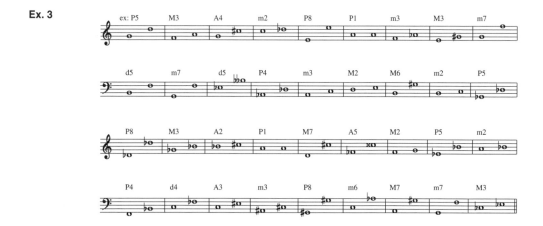

Appendix II: Solutions to Exercises

Chapter 4 cont'd...

Ex. 4

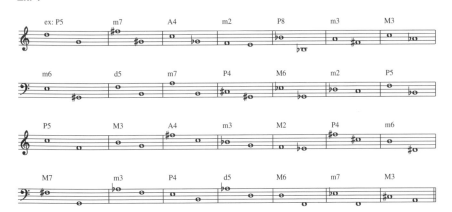

Ex. 5

(treble) P5, P1, P4, P8, m3, M3, d7, m7, M6;

(bass) M2, P4, m3, A5, m2, M7, d5, P4, d8;

(treble) A5, m2, m3, m7, A5, A5, A6, A5, d4;

(bass) M2, A2, d5, P8, A6, P8, A5, P4, P1

Chapter 5

Ex. 1 (treble) Fmi, C, G, Dmi, A, Emi; (bass) B, E♭mi, A♭mi, D♭, G♭, F♯

Ex. 2

Ex. 4 (treble) G+, F°, A♭+, F♯+; (bass) C♯+, A♭°, F+, B°

Ex. 5

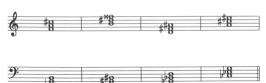

Ex. 3

Ex. 6

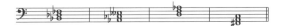

Ex. 7

Chapter 6

Ex. 6

Ex. 7

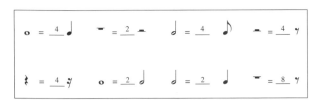

Ex. 8

Chapter 6 cont'd...

Ex. 9

Ex. 10

Ex. 11

Chapter 7

Ex. 1

Ex. 2

Appendix II: Solutions to Exercises

Chapter 7 cont'd...

Ex. 3

Ex. 4

Ex. 5

Chapter 8

Ex. 1

Ex. 2

Ex. 3

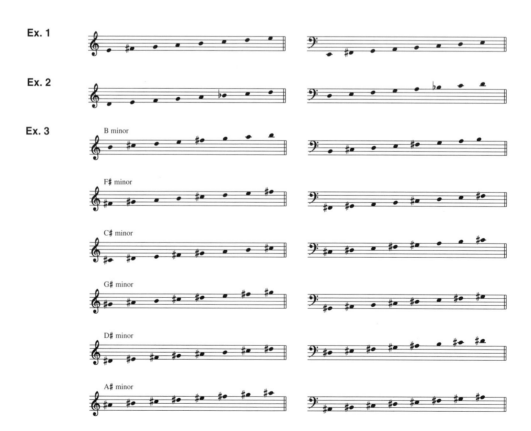

Chapter 8 cont'd...

Ex. 4

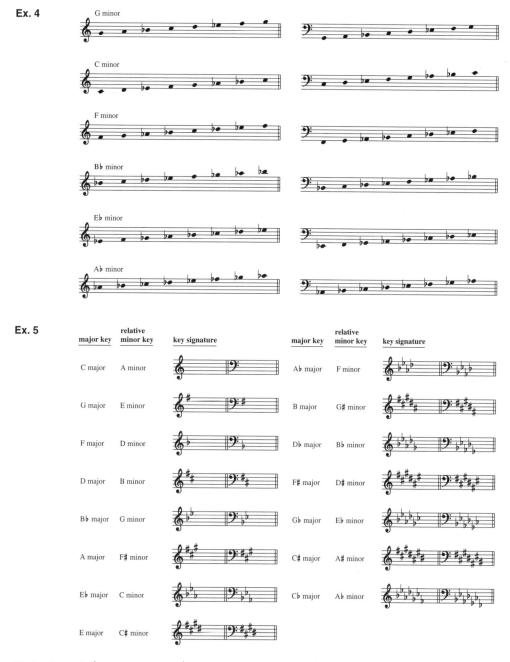

Ex. 5

major key	relative minor key	key signature		major key	relative minor key	key signature
C major	A minor			Ab major	F minor	
G major	E minor			B major	G# minor	
F major	D minor			Db major	Bb minor	
D major	B minor			F# major	D# minor	
Bb major	G minor			Gb major	Eb minor	
A major	F# minor			C# major	A# minor	
Eb major	C minor			Cb major	Ab minor	
E major	C# minor					

Ex. 6 (1st row) Bb major, D major, Gb major; (2nd row) A major, Eb major, G major; (3rd row) Ab major, E major, F major; (4th row) B major, Db major, C major

Ex. 7

Ex. 8

Appendix II: Solutions to Exercises

Chapter 9

Ex. 1

Ex. 2

Chapter 10

Ex. 1

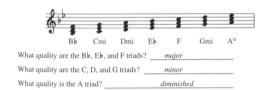

What quality are the Bb, Eb, and F triads? _____*major*_____

What quality are the C, D, and G triads? _____*minor*_____

What quality is the A triad? _____*diminished*_____

Ex. 2

↓ Keys ↓	I	IImi	IIImi	IV	V	VImi	VII°
C major	C	Dmi	Emi	F	G	Ami	B°
F major	F	Gmi	Ami	Bb	C	Dmi	E°
G major	G	Ami	Bmi	C	D	Emi	F#°
Bb major	Bb	Cmi	Dmi	Eb	F	Gmi	A°
D major	D	Emi	F#mi	G	A	Bmi	C#°
Eb major	Eb	Fmi	Gmi	Ab	Bb	Cmi	D°
A major	A	Bmi	C#mi	D	E	F#mi	G#°
Ab major	Ab	Bbmi	Cmi	Db	Eb	Fmi	G°
E major	E	F#mi	G#mi	A	B	C#mi	D#°
Db major	Db	Ebmi	Fmi	Gb	Ab	Bbmi	C°
B major	B	C#mi	D#mi	E	F#	G#mi	A#°

Ex. 3

1. (top to bottom, left to right) Ab, E, Emi, G°, D#mi, F#mi, Bmi, Gmi, Gmi, B, C°, F

2. F major, Ab major, E major, D major, Bb major, A major

3. D major, Gb major, E major, B major, Db major, Ab major

Ex. 4

1. C–F–G–C; F–Bb–C–F; G–C–D–C

2. Bb–Gmi–Cmi–F; D–Bmi–Emi–A; Eb–Cmi–Fmi–Bb

3. A–C#mi–F#mi–D; Ab–Cmi–Fmi–Db; E–G#mi–C#mi–A

Ex. 5

1. I–IV–V–I

2. I–VImi–IV–V

3. I–VImi–IImi–V

4. I–IIImi–VImi–IV

5. IIImi–VImi–IImi–V

Ex. 6

1. I–V–VImi–IV–VII°–IIImi–IImi–V;

   C–G–Ami–F–B°–Emi–Dmi–G

2. IV–I–V–VImi–IV–IIImi–IImi–V;

   F–C–G–Ami–F–Emi–Dmi–G

3. IIImi–IV–I–V–VII°–I–VImi–V;

   Emi–F–C–G–B°–C–Ami–G

Ex. 7

Appendix II: Solutions to Exercises

Chapter 11

Ex. 1

Gmi   A°   Bb   Cmi   Dmi   Eb   F

What quality are the G, C, and D triads? _____ *minor*

What quality are the Bb, Eb, and F triads? _____ *major*

What quality is the A triad? _____ *diminished*

Ex. 3 1. (left) Fmi, C#mi, C#o, Eb, B, D; (right) G, Gb, Eo, G#mi, Ab, Dmi

2. G minor, Bb minor; E minor, A minor; F# minor, B minor

3. E minor, Ab minor; F# minor, C# minor; Eb minor, Bb minor

Ex. 4 1. Gmi–Cmi–Gmi–Dmi; Cmi–Fmi–Gmi–Cmi; Dmi–Gmi–Ami–Dmi

2. Fmi–Db–Eb–Cmi; Ami–F–G–Emi; Bbmi–Gb–Ab–Fmi

3. F#mi–A–G#o–C#mi; C#mi–E–D#o–G#mi; Bmi–D–C#o–F#mi

Ex. 5 1. Imi–bVI–bIII–Vmi

2. Imi–IVmi–II°–Vmi

3. Imi–bIII–bVI–IVmi

4. Imi–Vmi–bVI–bVII

5. Imi–bVII–bIII–Vmi

Ex. 6 1. Imi–Vmi–bIII–IVmi–bVII–bIII–II°–Vmi;
Ami–Emi–C–Dmi–G–C–Bo–Emi

2. IVmi–Imi–Vmi–bVI–IVmi–bIII–II°–Vmi;
Dmi–Ami–Emi–F–Dmi–C–Bo–Emi

3. bIII–IVmi–Imi–Vmi–bVII–Imi–bVI–Vmi;
C–Dmi–Ami–Emi–G–Ami–F–Emi

Ex. 2

↓ Keys ↓	Imi	ii°	bIII	IVmi	Vmi	bVI	bVII
A minor	Ami	B°	C	Dmi	Emi	F	G
D minor	Dmi	E°	F	Gmi	Ami	Bb	C
E minor	Emi	F#°	G	Ami	Bmi	C	D
G minor	Gmi	A°	Bb	Cmi	Dmi	Eb	F
B minor	Bmi	C#°	D	Emi	F#mi	G	A
C minor	Cmi	D°	Eb	Fmi	Gmi	Ab	Bb
F# minor	F#mi	G#°	A	Bmi	C#mi	D	E
F minor	Fmi	G°	Ab	Bbmi	Cmi	Db	Eb
C# minor	C#mi	D#°	E	F#mi	G#mi	A	B
Bb minor	Bbmi	C°	Db	Ebmi	Fmi	Gb	Ab
G# minor	G#mi	A#°	B	C#mi	D#mi	E	F#

Chapter 12

Ex. 1

Ex. 5 1. C7, E7; B7, Ami7; Bmi7, Dmi7

2. Emi7, Bmi7; Gmi7, Fma7; Dbma7, Gma7

3. Fmi7, Bbmi; C#mi7, Dmi7(b5); G#mi7(b5), A#mi7(b5)

4. Dma7, Cma7; Abma7, Cmi7; Bbmi7, Fmi7

5. Ami7, F#mi7; Dmi7, Fma7; Gma7, Dma7

6. Gmi7(b5), A#mi7(b5); Bmi7(b5), E7; G7, F#7

Ex. 2

major triad   major 7th   dominant 7th   minor triad   minor 7th   diminished triad   minor 7th(b5)

Ex. 3

Bbma7   Eb7   C#mi7(b5)   Fmi7   E7   Ema7   Gmi7   Ami7(b5)

F#mi7(b5)   G#mi7   Dbma7   D7   Bmi7   Bb7   Gmi7(b5)   Ama7

Ex. 4

Cmi7   Dmi7(b5)   Ebma7   Fmi7   Gmi7   Abma7   Bb7

Chapter 13

Ex. 1 Eb major: Ima7–IVma7–VImi7–IImi7–V7–Ima7

Ex. 3 D minor: Imi7–bVII7–bVIma7–IImi7(b5)–V7–Imi7

Ex. 4 E–F#mi–G#mi–A–B–C#mi; I–IImi–IIImi–IV–V–Vimi

Ex. 2

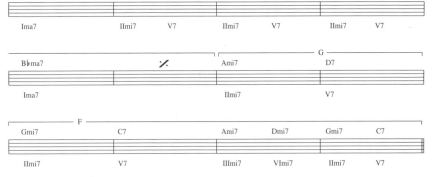

KEY:	F		D		C		Bb
Fma7		Emi7	A7	Dmi7	G7	Cmi7	F7
Ima7		IImi7	V7	IImi7	V7	IImi7	V7

			G	
Bbma7		✗	Ami7	D7
Ima7			IImi7	V7

	F			
Gmi7	C7	Ami7	Dmi7	Gmi7	C7
IImi7	V7	IIImi7	VImi7	IImi7	V7

Appendix II: Solutions to Exercises

Chapter 14

Ex. 1

Ex. 2

Ex. 3

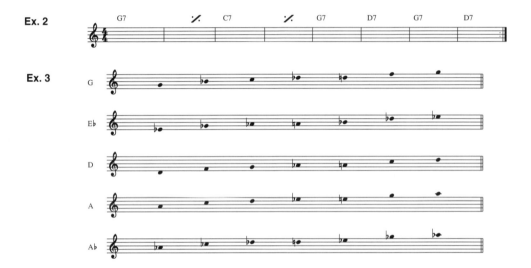

Chapter 15

Ex. 1

Ex. 2

Ex. 3   First inversion: D/F#, Bb+/D, E°/G, Gmi/Bb, F#/A#, A°/C, Ab+/C, Bmi/D

Second inversion: A+/E#, C°/Gb, Bbmi/F, Eb/Bb, B/F#, D°/Ab, C#mi/G#, E+/B#

Ex. 4

Chapter 15 cont'd...

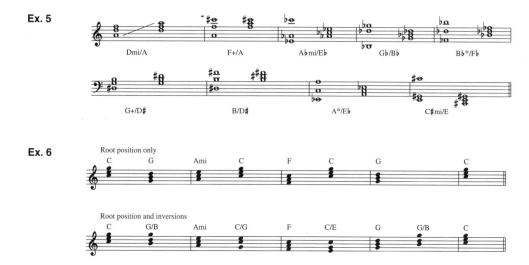

Ex. 5

Ex. 6

Chapter 16

Ex. 5 (treble) G13, B♭ma9, Ami11, Cma7(♯11), Ema9; (bass) F9, Dma9, E♭mi9, A♭ma7(♯11), Gmi13

Appendix II: Solutions to Exercises

Chapter 17

Ex. 2 (treble) Fsus, Dmi2, E♭6/9, E2, D♭mi6;

(bass) G5/2, B♭mi6/9 A7sus, A♭6, B5

Ex. 3 Cma7, Cmi7, C9, G♭ma7

Ex. 4 Cma9, Cmi11 (or C9sus), E9 (or Emi9)

Ex. 5 Ami–G/A–Ami; Imi–I9sus–Imi; Emi–G/A–D, IImi–V9sus–I

Ex. 6 F♯mi/C, C♯13(♯11/♭9); B/C, Cma7(♯11/♯9)

Ex. 7 $\dfrac{E♭}{C}$

Ex. 1

Chapter 18

Ex. 1

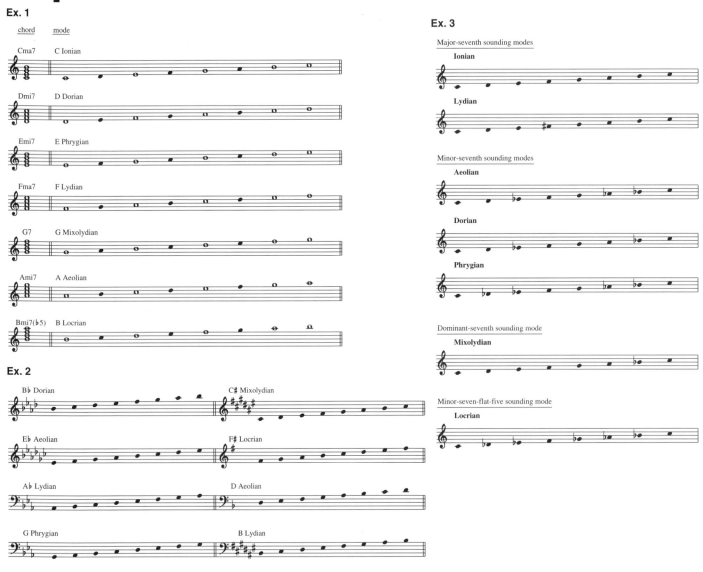

chord — mode

Cma7 — C Ionian

Dmi7 — D Dorian

Emi7 — E Phrygian

Fma7 — F Lydian

G7 — G Mixolydian

Ami7 — A Aeolian

Bmi7(♭5) — B Locrian

Ex. 2

B♭ Dorian — C♯ Mixolydian

E♭ Aeolian — F♯ Locrian

A♭ Lydian — D Aeolian

G Phrygian — B Lydian

Ex. 3

Major-seventh sounding modes

Ionian

Lydian

Minor-seventh sounding modes

Aeolian

Dorian

Phrygian

Dominant-seventh sounding mode

Mixolydian

Minor-seven-flat-five sounding mode

Locrian

Chapter 19

Ex. 1

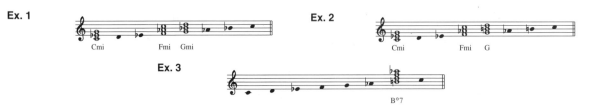

Cmi   Fmi Gmi

Ex. 2

Cmi   Fmi G

Ex. 3

B°7

Appendix II: Solutions to Exercises

Chapter 19 cont'd...

Ex. 4

Ex. 7

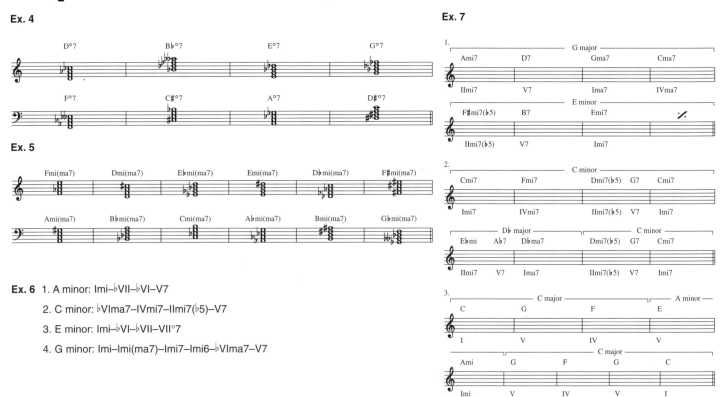

Ex. 5

Ex. 6 1. A minor: Imi–♭VII–♭VI–V7

2. C minor: ♭VIma7–IVmi7–IImi7(♭5)–V7

3. E minor: Imi–♭VI–♭VII–VII°7

4. G minor: Imi–Imi(ma7)–Imi7–Imi6–♭VIma7–V7

Chapter 20

Ex. 1

Ex. 3 A Dorian: Imi–IV7–Imi–IV7–
Imi–IImi–♭III–IV7–Imi–♭VII–Imi

Ex. 2

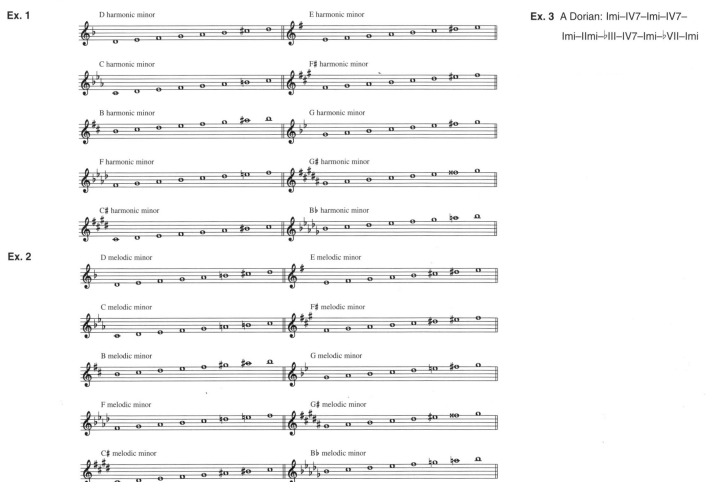

Appendix II: Solutions to Exercises

Chapter 21

Ex. 1

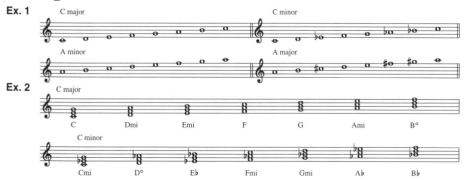

Ex. 2

Ex. 3 I–♭III–IV–♭VI–♭VII–I

Ex. 4 Imi–IV–♭VII–VII°–Imi

Ex. 5   1. G major: I–♭VII–I

2. D major: I–♭VII–IV–I–♭III–IImi–I

3. D minor: Imi–IV–Imi

4. B♭major: Ima7–VImi7–IImi7(♭5)–V7–
Ima7–VIm7–IVmi7–♭VII7–Ima7

Chapter 22

Ex. 2   1. I–V7/III–IIImi–V7/II–IImi–V7–I   2. Imi–Vmi–V7/♭III–♭III–IImi7(♭5)–V7–Imi   3. I–V7/IV–IV–IVmi–I   4. I–V7/V–V7–I

5. I–V7/VI–VImi–V7–I   6. Imi–V7/♭VI–♭VI–V7–Imi   7. Imi–V7/♭VII–♭VII–♭III–♭VI–IVmi–V7–Imi

Ex. 3   1. I–♭VI–V7/II–V7/V–V7–I   2. I–V7/VI–IV–I   3. I–V7/V–IV–I

4. I–V7/IV–♭III–IV–V–I   5. I–V7/V–IImi7–V7–I–I–V7/II–V7/V–V7–I–I–V7/VI–VImi–V7/IV–IV–IVmi–I

Chapter 23

Ex. 1

Ex. 4

1.

2.

Ex. 2 (top) B♭7(♭5), G7(♯9), A♭+9, A7(♭9); (bottom) D9(♭13), F9(♯11), E7(♭9), E♭9(♯11)

Ex. 3 C7–C+7–F; C7–C7(♭5)–F; C9–C7(♯9)–Fma7; C9–C7(♭9)–F; C7(♯11)–Fma7; C13–C7(♭13)–Fma9

Chapter 24

Ex. 2

Ex. 3 C7(♯11)

function: 1   9   3   ♯11   5   13   ♭7   (8)

Ex. 4 G Lydian ♭7 ... B♭ Lydian ♭7 ... E Lydian ♭7 ... F Lydian ♭7 ... E♭ Lydian ♭7 ... A Lydian ♭7

Ex. 1 F major: I6/9–VImi7–IImi9–V7($^{♭13}_{♭9}$)

Ex. 5 Lydian; melodic minor; Locrian

Ex. 6 Imi–Imi(ma7)[G melodic minor]–
Imi7–Imi6–♭VIma7–IVmi7–IImi7(♭5)–
V7($^{♭13}_{♭9}$) [D altered]–
Imi9–IVmi7–♭VII+7(♭9) [F altered]–
♭IIIma7–IVmi7–♭VII+7(♯9) [F altered]–
♭IIIma7–V7(♯11)/V [A♭Lydian ♭7]–
Imi7–IImi7(♭5)–V+7(♭9) [D altered]

Appendix II: Solutions to Exercises

Chapter 25

Ex. 1

Ex. 2 G7/B–C; B°7–C

Ex. 3 Ima7–VII°7/II–IImi7–VII°7/III–IIImi7

Ex. 4 Ima7–VII°7/II–IImi7–♯II°7–I

Ex. 5 Ima7–VII°7/II–IImi7–II°7–Ima7–V°7–IVma7–♯IV°7–I–V°7–IImi7–VII°7–Ima7–VII°7/II–IImi7–♯II°7–I

Chapter 26

Ex. 7 F major; G whole tone; G Dorian; C dominant diminished; F major

157

Appendix II: Solutions to Exercises

Chapter 27

Ex. 1 I, tonic, home; IV, subdominant, away; I, tonic, home; V, dominant, toward; I, tonic, home

Ex. 3 I–VImi–IIImi (tonic), IV–IImi (subdominant), I–VImi (tonic), V–VII° (dominant), I (tonic)

Ex. 5 Imi, tonic, home; IVmi, subdominant, away; Imi, tonic, home; Vmi, dominant, toward; Imi, tonic, home

Ex. 6 Imi–♭III–Imi–♭III (tonic), ♭VI–IVmi–II° (subdominant), ♭III–Imi (tonic), Vmi–♭VII (dominant), Imi (tonic)

Ex. 2

Ex. 4

Ex. 7

MAJOR KEY SUBSTITUTIONS

MINOR KEY SUBSTITUTIONS

Chapter 28

Ex. 1

What is the third of G7? B   What is the seventh of D♭7? C♭
What is the seventh of G7? F   What is the third of D♭7? F

Ex. 2 1. Ima7–VImi7–IImi7–♭II7–Ima7   2. IIImi7–VImi7–IImi7–♭II7–Ima7

Ex. 3 1. IIImi7–V7/II–IImi7–V7–Ima7

2. IIImi7–♭II7/II–IImi7–♭II7–Ima7

3. Imi–V7/IV–IVmi–IImi7(♭5)–V7–Imi

4. Imi–♭II7/IV–IVmi–IImi7(♭5)–♭II7–Imi

Chapter 29

Ex. 1 1. C major: I–V7–I–IVmi–I–IVmi–V7

A major: I–V7–I–IVmi–I–IVmi–V7–I

2. F major: I–IImi–V7–I–VImi–IImi–V7–I–V7

F♯ major: I–IImi–V7–I–VImi–IImi–V7–I

Ex. 2 1. C major: I–V7–I–IV–IImi–V7–IIImi (pivot chord)

D major: IImi–V7–I–IV–I–V7–I

2. C major: I–VImi–IV–V7–I–VImi (pivot chord)

E minor: IVmi–V7–Imi–IImi7(♭5)–V7–Imi

Ex. 3 1. A minor: Imi–IVmi–V7–Imi–♭VII–♭III (pivot chord)

E minor: ♭VI–V7–Imi–IVmi–V7–Imi

2. E♭ major: I–VImi–IV–V (direct modulation)

C major: I–IV–V7–I

158

Musicians Institute Press

is the official series of Southern California's renowned music school, Musicians Institute.

MI instructors, some of the finest musicians in the world, share their vast knowledge and experience with you – no matter what your current level.

For guitar, bass, drums, vocals, and keyboards, **MI Press** offers the finest music curriculum for higher learning through a variety of series:

FOR MORE INFORMATION, SEE YOUR LOCAL MUSIC DEALER, OR WRITE TO:

HAL•LEONARD®
CORPORATION

7777 W. BLUEMOUND RD. P.O. BOX 13819 MILWAUKEE, WI 53213

ESSENTIAL CONCEPTS

Designed from MI core curriculum programs.

Bass Fretboard Basics
by Paul Farnen
00695201 ....$12.95

Bass Playing Techniques
by Alexis Sklarevski
00695207 ....$12.95

Ear Training
by Keith Wyatt, Carl Schroeder, & Joe Elliot
00695198 Book/CD Pack $17.95

Guitar Soloing
by Dan Gilbert & Beth Marlis
00695190 Book/CD Pack $17.95

Harmony & Theory
by Keith Wyatt & Carl Schroeder
00695161 ....$14.95

Keyboard Voicings
by Kevin King
00695209 ....$14.95

Music Reading for Bass
by Wendy Wrehovcsik
00695203 ....$9.95

Music Reading for Guitar
by David Oakes
00695192 ....$14.95

Music Reading for Keyboard
by Larry Steelman
00695205 ....$14.95

Rhythm Guitar
by Bruce Buckingham & Eric Paschal
00695188 Book/CD Pack $16.95

Sightsinging
by Mike Campbell
00695195 ....$16.95

MASTER CLASS

Designed from MI elective courses.

An Approach to Jazz Improvisation
by Dave Pozzi
00695135 Book/CD Pack $17.95

Blues Bass
by Alexis Sklarevski
00695150 Book/CD Pack $17.95

Guitar Playing Techniques
by David Oakes
00695171 ....$12.95

Jazz Guitar Improvisation
by Sid Jacobs
00695128 Book/CD Pack $17.95

Rock Lead Basics
by Danny Gill & Nick Nolan
00695144 Book/CD Pack $14.95

Rock Lead Guitar Techniques
by Nick Nolan & Danny Gill
00695146 Book/CD Pack $14.95

Walking Bass
by Bob Magnusson
00695168 Book/CD Pack $17.95

PRIVATE LESSONS

Tackle a variety of topics "one-on-one" with MI faculty instructors.

Arpeggios for Bass
by Dave Keif
00695133 ....$12.95

Blues Rhythm Guitar
by Steve Trovato
00695180 Book/CD Pack $12.95

Chart Reading Workbook for Drummers
by Bobby Gabriele
00695129 Book/CD Pack $14.95

Creative Chord Shapes
by Jamie Findlay
00695172 Book/CD Pack $7.95

Diminished Scale for Guitar
by Jean Marc Belkadi
00695227 Book/CD Pack $9.95

Encyclopedia of Reading Rhythms
by Gary Hess
00695145 ....$19.95

Guitar Basics
by Bruce Buckingham
00695134 Book/CD Pack $14.95

Harmonics for Guitar
by Jamie Findlay
00695169 Book/CD Pack $7.95

Lead Sheet Bible
by Robin Randall
00695130 Book/CD Pack $19.95

Modern Approach to Jazz, Rock & Fusion Guitar
by Jean March-Belkadi
00695143 Book/CD Pack $12.95

Odd-Meter Bassics
by Dino Monoxelos
00695170 Book/CD Pack $14.95

Salsa Hanon
by Peter Deneff
00695226 ....$9.95

Working the Inner Clock for Drumset
by Phil Maturano
00695127 Book/CD Pack $10.95

Prices, contents, and availability subject to change without notice. Some products may not be available outside of the U.S.A.

0198